Naval Aces of World War 1

Part 1

SERIES EDITOR: TONY HOLMES

OSPREY AIRCRAFT OF THE ACES • 97

Naval Aces of World War 1
Part 1

Jon Guttmann

OSPREY
PUBLISHING

Front Cover
At 2040 hrs on 11 August 1917, Flt Lt Charles D Booker of 8 Naval Squadron, Royal Naval Air Service (RNAS), was leading Flt Sub-Lts Stanley W McCrudden, Charles H B Jenner-Parsons and Reginald R Soar on an evening patrol. Jenner-Parsons dived on an enemy aeroplane, and shortly thereafter the remaining three Sopwith Triplanes chanced upon a dogfight involving six Nieuports, six SE 5as and ten Albatros D Vs.

'I turned off right, saw McCrudden dive left, and I took after the last Hun', Soar subsequently wrote. 'Booker went straight after the first scout he could get at, and as I turned back I saw he had fastened onto a black Hun that was going down with its engine fully open and smoke spewing out of the cockpit – it was obviously on fire. Good old "Bookie"'. Booker's quarry was a frequent nemesis of the RNAS pilots, Hptm Adolf *Ritter* von Tutschek, commander of *Jasta* 12 and then victor over 22 Allied aeroplanes. He later wrote about what happened to him as he was pursuing an SE 5a;

'I am in the midst of aiming when I suffer a jammed loading chamber. In the same instant there is a hit in front of me, and the radiator is ruptured. Hot water splashes in my face, and I can't see a thing. The aircraft is enshrouded in a white steam cloud. With the right hand (I briefly fly the machine with my left hand), off with the goggles. I see the triplane, who thinks he has set me on fire, head straight as an arrow toward me. His phosphorus and tracer bullets whistle around my ears and register hits all over my machine. I am about to answer his fire when there is a terrific blow to my right shoulder. The stick with my lifeless arm falls into the corner and the aeroplane tumbles over, spinning downward. I lose consciousness.'

Von Tutschek came to at 1600 ft, six kilometres inside Allied territory, with Booker still on his tail. 'Suddenly', he continued, 'something very unexpected happens. A comrade has recognised my desperate situation. He dives and attacks the triplane from above, and after a few shots has him going down. Now my spirit soars again. I turn on the ignition and the motor kicks on. At an altitude of 150 metres I crawl home over our lines in the direction of Henin-Liétard.'

Booker was driven down near Farbus by Ltn d R Viktor Schobinger, becoming his second of six victories. The RNAS pilot emerged unhurt, but his distinctively marked Triplane, N5482, was subsequently destroyed by artillery fire, as described by Soar;

'There were two machines under Booker's tail. As I shook off my first chap I could only reach the last one behind Booker, driving him off. Not watching the Hun on fire, I did not see him crash, but "Bookie" himself was flopping about now, and at almost ground height I saw him spread out near Farbus, which Jerry started to shell at once. That was the end of Booker's last triplane. Now for those damned Camels' (*Cover artwork by M Postlethwaite*)

First published in Great Britain in 2011 by Osprey Publishing
Midland House, West Way, Botley, Oxford, OX2 0PH
44-02 23rd Street, Suite 219, Long Island City, NY, 11101, USA

E-mail; info@ospreypublishing.com

ISBN 13: 978 1 84908 345 4
E-book ISBN: 978 1 84908 346 1

Edited by Tony Holmes
Page design by Tony Truscott
Cover Artwork by Mark Postlethwaite
Aircraft Profiles by Harry Dempsey
Index by Alan Thatcher
Originated by PDQ Digital Media Solutions
Printed and bound in China through Bookbuilders

11 12 13 14 15   10 9 8 7 6 5 4 3 2 1

Osprey Publishing is supporting the Woodland Trust, the UK's leading woodland conservation charity by funding the dedication of trees.

www.ospreypublishing.com

ACKNOWLEDGEMENTS
I wish to acknowledge the invaluable help provided by the following colleagues in the scavenger hunt for both information and photographs for inclusion in this book – Jack Eder, Colin Huston, Norman Franks, Andrew Kemp, George Stuart Leslie, Les Rogers, Stewart Taylor, Mike Westrop and Greg VanWyngarden. Posthumous thanks are also extended to W M Alexander, Alfred W 'Nick' Carter, E R Grange, Edmund Pierce and Leonard H Rochford, whose recollections gave me a somewhat better understanding of the first air war as they experienced it. This book is dedicated to them, their mates and to the memory of Henry Allingham, the very last of the breed.

CONTENTS

SENIOR SERVICE TAKES WING

When Henry Allingham died on 18 July 2009, an era went with him. Aged 113 at the time of his death, he was one of the last British veterans of World War 1, as well as being the very last to have seen active duty in an air arm that presaged the Royal Air Force (RAF) – the Royal Naval Air Service (RNAS). Enlisting as an air mechanic in 1915, Allingham had serviced and helped launch floatplanes. In 1917 he joined 12 Naval Squadron, which later became No 212 Sqn RAF, and in the war's last year he manned a Lewis machine gun as an observer in DH 4s and DH 9As during bombing missions.

Allingham was the last, but by no means only, member of the RNAS to make headlines. Although sometimes regarded as a 'junior partner' to the British Army's Royal Flying Corps (RFC), the air arm of the 'Senior Service' played a significant role throughout the conflict until its assimilation in the RAF on 1 April 1918. That included fighter units that were as well, if not better, equipped than their RFC partners and a galaxy of distinguished fighter pilots to match the RFC's best – Raymond Collishaw, Robert Little, Roderic Stanley Dallas and C D Booker to name but a few.

The RFC and RNAS were both founded in 1912. 'The RNAS was then known officially as the Naval Wing of the RFC', recalled one of its leading aces, Leonard H 'Titch' Rochford, 'and it was not until mid-summer 1914 (just before World War 1) that they both became separate services. But, unofficially, the Royal Navy had a flying unit at Eastchurch under Cdr C R Samson in which it trained its own pilots independently of the RFC'.

Both services had experimented with arming aircraft before war broke out, trying to solve the problem of firing a machine gun from a fast-moving single-seat tractor scout without riddling the propeller. Free from such issues, two-seat pusher aircraft were also armed with a gun in the nacelle. In the RNAS's case, Lewis guns were frequently installed in Sopwith Tabloids and Bristol Scouts, either firing directly through the airscrew – playing the odds against likely damage – or above the upper wing. In July 1914 the RNAS ordered six Sopwith Gun Buses – two-seat pushers with a flexible gun mount for the forward observer. At least one was operated from Dunkirk with Cdr Charles Rumney Samson's Eastchurch Squadron in February 1915. Samson commented that it took 'a lot of work on it to make it safe to fly', and the Gun Bus was soon relegated to the training role.

In July 1915 Nieuport 10 two-seat sesquiplanes acquired from the French began operating over the Dardanelles, and they were joined in August by Bristol Scouts. Both types were armed with single overwing Lewis guns. When Nieuport introduced a smaller single-seat version

Enlisting in the RNAS in 1915, Henry Allingham served as an air mechanic aboard His Majesty's Trawler *Kingfisher*, servicing and helping launch its Sopwith Schneider floatplane during the Battle of Jutland on 31 May 1916. By 1918 he had become an observer/gunner in DH 4 and DH 9A bombers of No 212 Sqn RAF (*Cross & Cockade International*)

of the 10 – the 11 *Bébé* – the RNAS ordered substantial numbers from November 1915.

The introduction of these machines could not come soon enough for the Allies, as a few months earlier the Germans had unleashed the 'Fokker Scourge' – an onslaught of single-seat monoplanes equipped with mechanical interrupter gear that released the machine gun trigger every time the propeller passed in front of the muzzle. The stage was set for a struggle for control of the skies in which the naval air arms of both sides would become as earnestly involved as their army colleagues.

NIMBLE NIEUPORTS

By the late summer of 1915 the RNAS had six squadrons, two of which were fighter units, in the Dunkirk area, as well as two in Dover. All were under the command of Wing Captain Charles L Lambe. At that time what the RFC called a squadron the RNAS called a wing, whose six-aeroplane squadrons in turn corresponded to an RFC flight. By December Lambe had obtained the Admiralty's approval to form two more wings, each comprising four squadrons. Their purpose, as he conceived it, was threefold – protect supply routes across the English Channel to the British Expeditionary Force, harass enemy submarines and take offensive action against German forces along the Channel coast.

One of Lambe's Dunkirk-based units, 1 Naval Wing, was posted to St Pol-sur-Mer, where its regular duties of coastal reconnaissance and bombing German bases such as Ostend and Zeebrugge were supplemented by intercepting Zeppelin airships. The wing's 'A' Naval Squadron was a fighter element, equipped with Nieuport 10s and 11s.

The status of the first RNAS ace is somewhat an article of faith, since this achievement was attained at a time when such vagaries as 'forced to land' and 'out of control' (OOC) were accepted more readily than they would later be. Taking this into account, the first RNAS member – and the first Canadian – to achieve ace status was Redford Henry Mulock, for whom it was almost an incidental distinction.

Born in Winnipeg, Alberta, on 11 August 1886, 'Red' Mulock (a sobriquet derived from his name, not his hair) was the son of a barrister. After graduating from McGill University he became a lieutenant in the 13th Canadian Field Artillery in 1911, but when war broke out he forsook his commission for a corporal's rank to expedite his passage to the front. In January 1915 Mulock transferred to the RNAS on home defence. Patrolling in an Avro 504 on the night of 16-17 May, he attacked airship *LZ38* over the Thames. Unfortunately for him – but fortunately for the startled Germans – his gun jammed after a few rounds, allowing the Zeppelin crew to drop ballast and escape.

In July Mulock was assigned to 1 Naval Wing at St Pol. In a letter to his parents dated 6 October 1915, he wrote that generally 'the war is rather monotonous and we are

The world's oldest man at the time of his death on 18 July 2009, Allingham, who was 113, was also one of the last surviving British veterans of World War 1 as well as the last to have seen active service in the RNAS (*Cross & Cockade International*)

An unidentified pilot of 1 Naval Wing sits astride Nieuport 11 N593 (British serial number 3981) at St Pol-sur-Mer in 1916. Later assigned to 'Naval 6', this aircraft was struck by ground fire and its pilot, Flt Sub-Lt George P Powles, forced to crash-land in Cadzand, Zeeland, on 26 February 1917. The Dutch authorities interned Powles and used his aeroplane as a template for their own licence-produced version of the French scout (*Fleet Air Arm Museum JMB/GSL09409*)

Lt Redford H Mulock served in the 13th Canadian Field Battery at Valcartier, Quebec, in August 1914. When war broke out, he resigned his commission to expedite his passage to the front as a member of the RNAS (*Stewart K Taylor*)

Queenslander Roderic Stanley Dallas poses for the camera in his RNAS uniform whilst undergoing training in late 1915 (*Norman Franks*)

all pretty tired of it', but he did mention some exceptions;

'I was patrolling over the monitor fleet when this German came over to drop bombs. I succeeded in driving him in under his guns at Zeebrugge in a rather bad condition. He fought gamely though, and had a good many holes in my machine to his credit.

'Another time I dropped a few bombs on a submarine who went down, never to come up again I hope. He stayed on top and returned my fire from two Maxims. I was only 400 ft above him, so you can see it was fairly hot work.'

This action occurred on 6 September, Mulock conducting the first aerial attack on a U-boat. The five 20-lb bombs that he dropped failed to destroy the vessel, however.

'Then I flew to Brussels in broad daylight and dropped some bombs on a new Zepp shed', he continued. 'It was a very hard trip. I was continually fired at all the way from Dixmude, when I crossed the lines into Brussels, and back. Outside of that it has been for the most part ordinary work, reconnaissance, fighting, patrols, sea patrols, photographing, bomb-dropping and any odd jobs that turn up.'

On 30 December Flt Sub-Lt Mulock scored his first official victory with a two-seater OOC near the Houthulst Forest. Flying Nieuport 3977, he forced a two-seater to land near Westende on 24 January 1916 and downed another OOC near the town of Nieuport two days later.

Mulock was not alone in aggressive zeal. On 25 January 24-year-old Flt Sub-Lt Noel Keeble, in Nieuport 3178, forced a floatplane to alight at sea. On 20 February, Flt Lt Roderic Stanley Dallas drove down a two-seater that was not confirmed.

Born in Mount Stanley, Queensland on 30 July 1891, Dallas was commissioned in the Australian Army in 1913, but applied to the RFC when war broke out. His application was turned down, but the RNAS readily accepted him, and after commencing training in May 1915, Dallas joined 1 Naval Wing on 3 December. His first official victory came on 22 April 1916 in the form of a two-seater OOC near Middelkerke. On 20 May he destroyed a floatplane off Blankenberghe.

On 21 May Mulock, flying Nieuport 3992, 'made ace' with two enemy two-seaters OOC off Nieuport, while Dallas downed another north of Dunkirk. In June

Flt Lt Dallas with a Nieuport 11 *Bébé* of 1 Naval Wing at St Pol-sur-Mer. He scored his first official victory (a two-seater OOC) in Nieuport 3987 on 22 April 1916. On 20 May Dallas destroyed a floatplane flying 3993, followed by a two-seater OOC in 3991 the very next day (*Norman Franks*)

Mulock was gazetted for the Distinguished Service Order (DSO), as much for his relentless bombing activities as for his aerial combats. That same month 'A' Naval Squadron was moved closer to the front, at Furnes, and furnished solely with single-seat Nieuports. Known as the 'Detached Squadron', it was the RNAS's first uniformly equipped unit.

On 8 July Flt Sub-Lt Thomas Francis Netterville Gerrard, flying Nieuport 3889, downed a Fokker monoplane OOC off Ostend. Born on 30 August 1897 as the son of Brig E L Gerrard DSO, 'Teddy' Gerrard enlisted in the RNAS in 1915, arrived at the Dunkirk Seaplane Base that December and joined 'A' Naval Squadron on 10 June 1916.

In late June 'A' Squadron received its first Sopwith Pups and, for a few months, the first prototype Sopwith Triplane (N500) too, which Dallas used to score a victory on 1 July. Eight days later, after reverting to Nieuport 3994, he downed a Fokker E III OOC near Mariakerke.

On 15 July a sometime rival of Mulock's for the title of 'first Canadian ace', Flt Sub-Lt Daniel Murray Bayne Galbraith, claimed a floatplane in flames off Ostend. Born in Carleton Place, Ontario, on 27 April 1895, Galbraith had learned to fly in the United States before joining the RNAS in 1915.

Another budding Australian ace made his debut on 21 July when 25-year-old Flt Sub-Lt Stanley James Goble, from Croyden, Victoria, used Nieuport 8517 to down a two-seater OOC east of Ostend. He destroyed a floatplane whilst at the controls of the same Nieuport on 15 August.

Galbraith, in Nieuport 3992, destroyed a floatplane off Calais on 28 September. Two days later, Dallas scored again in Triplane N500. He was then posted to Cranwell as an instructor, but rejoined 'A' Naval Squadron, since redesignated 1 Naval Squadron, as a flight leader in December.

On 20 October Flt Sub-Lt Ernest William Norton, flying Nieuport 3994, used wing-mounted Le Prieur rockets to destroy a kite balloon over Ostend, for which he was awarded the Distinguished Service Cross

Lt Noel Keeble and his observer, Capt Eric B C Betts, sit third and fourth from left among crewmen of No 202 Sqn RAF in 1918, by which point they had raised their respective tallies to six and five in DH 4 A7446. Keeble scored his first two victories with 1 Naval Wing, while Betts got his first in a Sopwith 1½ Strutter of 'Naval 2' (*N Franks*)

Flt Lt John W Alcock of 'E' Flight, 2 Naval Wing, stands before newly arrived Triplane N5431 at Mikra Bay airfield, Stavros, near Salonika, in January 1917. Alcock ran the aeroplane into a ditch on 26 March, but it had been restored to airworthiness by mid-May (*Fleet Air Arm Museum JMB/GSL06491*)

(DSC). Born in Montgomery, Powys, on 14 May 1893, Norton would soon add eight more successes to that fiery debut.

23 October saw Keeble double his score when, flying Pup 5183, he destroyed a floatplane off Ostend. Almost two years later, whilst flying DH 4 bombers with No 202 Sqn RAF, Lt Keeble and his observer, Capt E B C Betts, scored four more victories. Keeble, who had received the DSO following his second victory, was presented with the Distinguished Flying Cross (DFC) and Bar in the wake of his fifth (Pfalz D III) and sixth (Fokker D VII) victories on 16 September 1918.

Born in Dublin on 24 January 1897, Betts had been a signalman in the Royal Navy Volunteer Reserve prior to becoming an observer with 1 Naval Wing. He downed an Albatros D II OOC on 1 February 1917 in a Sopwith 1½ Strutter while serving with 2 Naval Squadron, and was awarded the DSC and the French *Croix de Guerre* (CdG) with Palm. Raising his tally to five with Keeble as his DH 4 pilot, he received the DFC. Betts remained in the RAF postwar, and during World War 2 he became an acting air vice-marshal and was made a Commander in the Order of the British Empire (CBE). He died on 30 October 1971.

As the war expanded, so did the RNAS's commitments beyond the Western Front. This included the Eastern Mediterranean, where 2 Naval Wing operated from Imbros and other Aegean islands in support of Allied forces in Salonika and the Dardanelles.

One of its pilots, Flt Sub-Lt Harold Thomas Mellings, was born in Shropshire on 5 August 1897, and he used a Bristol Scout to down

an LVG OOC near Smyrna on 30 September 1916. Exactly a year later, two Albatros W 4 floatplane fighters newly delivered to the German navy's *Wasserfliegerabteilung* at Chanak Kale (Canakkale) were escorting a reconnaissance aeroplane over Mudros Bay, on Lemnos Island, when they were both shot down by Mellings. He was flying the wing's sole Sopwith Triplane, N5431, while Flt Lt John W Alcock was in a new Sopwith Camel. Flgobmt Walter Krüger was killed, while the fate of his unidentified wingman was described by RNAS Capt Augustine F Marlowe. 'We have been showing a Hun prisoner around. He was forced down in the sea and we picked him up. He seems quite a nice bloke and very friendly'.

Mellings enjoyed a scoring streak in November 1917, with an Albatros D III on the 19th (wounding Vfw van Ahlen of FA 30), a Rumpler in flames over Drama on the 25th and another D III four days later. Awarded the DSC and the Hellenic Silver War Medal, Mellings would subsequently see further action over the Western Front in 1918.

3 Naval Wing also moved to the Aegean in 1915. While there, its ranks included Samuel Marcus Kinkead, a South African born in Johannesburg on 25 February 1897 who had joined the RNAS in September 1915. Flying a Bristol Scout, he drove down an Eindecker over Xanthi on 22 August 1916. Switching to a Nieuport, he forced a two-seater to land northwest of Zinelli on the 28th and was later credited with a third victory. Shipped to England, he was posted to No 1 Sqn in June 1917.

While the RNAS's first fighter pilots were being blooded over Flanders, as of 1 July 1916 the RFC was engaged in the Battle of the Somme, where its mixed bag of tractor and pusher fighters broke the supremacy of the Fokker monoplane and biplane fighters. In September 1916, however, the introduction of the twin-gun Albatros D I and D II, along with specialised *Jagdstaffeln* or *Jastas*, and their tactical use in accordance with Hptm Oswald Boelcke's dicta, led to a disturbing rise

The rebuilt Triplane N5431, with a Lewis gun added, is seen here serving with 'C' Flight of 2 Naval Wing at Imbros, on the island of Lemnos. Flt Sub-Lt H T Mellings scored four of his five victories over the Aegean in this aeroplane (*Fleet Air Arm Museum JMB/GSL06493*)

Flt Sub-Lt Mellings was the RNAS' top scorer in the eastern Mediterranean, later adding to his tally over the Western Front prior to being killed in action while serving with No 210 Sqn RAF on 22 July 1918 (*Mike Westrop*)

During 3 Naval Wing's time in the Aegean, South African Flt Sub-Lt Samuel Marcus Kinkead claimed a Fokker Eindecker while flying a Bristol Scout and two victories in Nieuports during August 1916. Later serving with 1 Naval Squadron and No 201 Sqn RAF, he would bring his total up to 33 on 13 August 1918. Kinkead subsequently added two more victories over Russia in 1919 (*Norman Franks*)

Lt Col Mulock is highlighted above personnel of his last wartime command, the 27th Group, and a Handley Page V/1500 of No 166 Sqn at Bircham Newton. The unit was declared ready to carry out night bombing operations against Berlin just three days before the armistice was signed (*Stewart K Taylor*)

in losses. In consequence, the RFC's commander, Maj Gen Hugh M Trenchard, informally approached Capt Lambe to request that RNAS fighter units be shifted south and one attached to each British army on the Western Front.

As of 20 November, the RNAS wings were restructured and expanded along RFC lines to form seven squadrons, along with a new unit, 8 Naval Squadron. In December, 'A' Naval Squadron was redesignated 1 Naval Squadron and commenced the replacement of its Nieuports with Sopwith Triplanes, while the balance of 1 Naval Wing became a supply and administration body. In addition, 3, 4, 6 and 8 Naval Squadrons were to be fighter units.

In January 1917 Flt Lt Mulock was given command of the newly formed 3 Naval Squadron. 'He was older than most of us, and I was at once impressed by his strong personality', recalled one of his young pilots, Leonard Rochford. 'A man of medium height, he had a square, weatherbeaten face with eyes that nearly always had a twinkle in them. Later, I was to discover that he was a highly competent organiser and had a deep understanding of human nature'.

Although he scored no further victories, Mulock's outstanding leadership earned him a Bar to his DSO and, on 14 September, French honours as a *Chevalier de la Légion d'Honneur*. By war's end he was a wing commander, and the highest-ranking Canadian officer in the RAF. Mulock went on to serve in the Royal Canadian Air Force (RCAF), retiring as an air commodore in 1935 to join Canadian Airways. Mulock died on 23 January 1961.

Although most of the RNAS squadrons were equipped with Sopwiths, 6 Naval Squadron, formed from 'A' Naval Squadron of 4 Naval Wing at Petite Synthe and transferred on 11 March 1917 to serve under the command of No 13 Wing, 3rd Brigade, RFC at La Bellevue aerodrome, retained its Nieuports. By then the Nieuport 17bis, powered by a 110 hp Le Rhône engine, was replacing the 80 hp *Bébé*, along with a glimpse of things to come in the form of the prototype Sopwith F 1 Camel, which was briefly on hand for squadron evaluation.

One of 'Naval 6's' first victories in the newer Nieuports was scored by Flt Lt William Norton when, on 8 February, he sent an Aviatik down smoking over the Houthulst Forest. He was credited with an OOC.

When 6 Naval Squadron began serious operations in support of the British Arras offensive on 4 April 1917, its pilots faced the same formidable opposition as their RFC comrades-in-arms. The Germans, impressed by the manoeuvrability and excellent downward visibility of the Nieuport sesquiplanes, had introduced such a wing arrangement in the Albatros to produce the D III. Flown by seasoned disciples of Oswald Boelcke – who had been killed in a mid-air collision on 28 October 1916 – the D IIIs proved deadly adversaries in spite of the fact that they, more than the Nieuports, displayed the limitations of the sesquiplane structure, whose single-spar lower wing had a tendency to vibrate and break up during high-speed dives.

On 5 April Norton claimed a D III in flames and another OOC west of Douai, while Flt Sub-Lt Alfred L Thorne also claimed an enemy aircraft OOC. On the debit side, Flt Sub-Lt Robert K Slater was brought down (possibly by Vfw Karl Menckhoff of *Jasta* 3) and captured. Four days later, Norton and Thorne sent a scout crashing to earth near Cambrai, Norton following this success up a short while later when he downed an Albatros OOC. Those victories were dampened later that same day when stormy conditions caused three Nieuports to crash, killing Thorne and injuring Norton and Flt Sub-Lt John de C Paynter.

Less than satisfied with 'Naval 6's' overall performance, No 13 Wing had it transferred to Chipilly on 11 April for attachment to No 14 Wing, 4th Brigade. Its place was taken by Triplane-equipped 1 Naval Squadron. Among the replacement pilots assigned to 'Naval 6' on 22 April was Sqn Cdr Christopher Draper, a veteran with four previous victories to his name in Sopwith 1½ Strutters whilst flying with 3 Naval Wing.

On 29 April Norton and Flt Sub-Lt Albert H V Fletcher downed an Albatros OOC east of Honnecourt. Leading a later patrol, Norton was attacked over Harcourt and, turning to engage his opponent head-on, claimed it in flames, followed by a second D III OOC. Attacked by a third persistent adversary, Norton landed in German territory and then, as the Albatros shot past him, took off again. Racing along at an altitude of just 100 ft, with the German again in pursuit of him, Norton managed to cross the lines and reach home.

Nieuport 17bis scouts of 'Naval 6' line up at Chipilly aerodrome. Flt Lt Christopher Draper's Nieuport N3101, bearing the two red bands that signified his leadership of 'B' Flight, can be seen at right (*Les Rogers Collection via Mike Westrop*)

Replacement pilots for 'Naval 6' drafted in from 'Naval 11' included, from left, back row, Flt Sub-Lts Stearnes T Edwards, Norman M Macgregor, Percy E Beasley and George L E Stevens and Flt Lt Christopher Draper. In the front row, Flt Sub-Lt Ronald F Redpath and Flt Lt G G MacLennan flank Draper's dog 'Joey'. Draper, previously credited with four victories during bombing missions in Sopwith 1½ Strutters with 3 Naval Wing, downed two enemy aircraft with 'Naval 6' on 6 June 1917 just after the decision had been made to transfer him out as being detrimental to unit morale! Returning to combat with 'Naval 8', Draper scored thrice more in Camels and finished the war as a 'Mad Major' in the RAF (*Mike Westrop*)

After burning a German kite balloon while serving in 1 Naval Wing on 20 October 1916, Flt Lt Ernest W Norton claimed eight more victories with 'Naval 6', including two doubles and a 'hat trick' (*Norman Franks*)

Flt Sub-Lt Rupert Randolph Winter, a North Londoner from Woodside Park who had turned 21 five days earlier, also came under attack during the same engagement. After turning on one opponent in a vertical bank, he was about to open fire when his Nieuport and the Albatros both fell into vertical spins. Winter, who recovered at 1000 ft, claimed to have seen his opponent crash. He then recrossed the lines under heavy anti-aircraft fire.

Fletcher was less fortunate, being brought down with a calf wound and taken prisoner. His demise was credited to Ltn Hermann Göring of *Jasta* 26. Göring's report of what followed his success over '2Lt Fletscher' suggests that he in turn was almost certainly Norton's ninth, and final, victory;

'When I flew at a height of 100 m to Bohain, a second enemy single-seater approached me from above, chased by an Albatros. The Britisher attacked me and hit my lateral control. He himself was then pursued by an Albatros and forced to land. I could not observe any further developments since I had to fly without lateral control, which demanded my whole attention.'

On 14 May Norton was transferred to command newly formed 12 Naval Squadron. He would subsequently lead 'Naval 9' and No 204 Sqn RAF in 1918, surviving the war with the Belgian Order of the Crown as well as the French and Belgian CdG. Serving in Iraq from 1924 to 1926, Norton had been promoted to group captain by 1932 and placed in charge of No 5 Flying Training School. He retired from the RAF as an air commodore in 1944.

After losing its best Nieuport pilot to 'Naval 12', 6 Naval Squadron saw the debut of another ace on 20 May when Flt Lt Bruno Philip Henry de Roeper drove an Albatros two-seater down OOC northwest of Bohain. Born in Forest Gate, London, on 22 March 1892, de Roeper had flown anti-Zeppelin patrols prior to joining 'Naval 6'. As he dived on another two-seater on 25 May, the observer's return fire struck him in the lower jaw and severed the Bowden cable to his overhead Lewis gun. Disengaging, de Roeper would not return to his squadron until July, by which time it had re-equipped with Camels. He would subsequently claim four more victories with the Sopwith fighter.

Flt Sub-Lt Bruno P H de Roeper opened his account with 'Naval 6' by sending a two-seater down OOC on 20 May 1917, but he was wounded while attacking another five days later. He subsequently rejoined the squadron and achieved acedom flying Camels in July-August 1917 (*Mike Westrop*)

Draper was leading eight Nieuport 17bis in conjunction with Pups of No 54 Sqn as escorts for FE 2bs of No 22 Sqn on 6 June when they encountered a large force of German aeroplanes northwest of Cambrai. In the ensuing melée Draper claimed a Albatros OOC and, after clearing a gun jam, sent another crashing before a second jam forced him to abandon further action. 'Naval 6' lost Flt Lt Fabian P Reeves, who was killed by Ltn Werner Voss of *Jasta* 5. Voss in turn landed with wounds, suggesting that Draper had indeed meted out some revenge after all.

In spite of his success, Draper was relieved of his command on 11 June and sent home to command the Eastchurch War Flight. Among other reasons for the transfer, Capt Lambe's report included the comments 'Very little idea of discipline, but a brilliant pilot. Good command when he cares to exercise it, but is too inclined to be boisterous. A very bad example to young pilots'.

In July 'Naval 6' moved to Bray Dunes and resumed operations with Camels, in which its pilots – especially Bruno de Roeper – would raise its overall score to 35 by 27 August, when the unit was disbanded and its Sopwiths passed on to 10 Naval Squadron. 'Naval 6' was re-formed in January 1918, but as a bomber unit, and it flew DH 4s and DH 9s for the balance of the war as No 206 Sqn RAF.

A veteran of bomber operations with 3 Naval Wing, Flt Sub-Lt Edwards arrived at 'Naval 6' on 19 April 1917 and made his first flight in Nieuport 17bis N3200 four days later, only to be forced to make an embarrassing landing due to a faulty fuel line. Although failing to score with his new unit, Edwards would subsequently go on to claim eight victories with 'Naval 9' and another eight with No 209 Sqn RAF (*Les Rogers Collection via Mike Westrop*)

SENSIBLE SOPWITHS

The havoc wrought on two-seater reconnaissance aeroplanes by Fokker Eindeckers over the Western Front during the summer of 1915 elicited two responses from the British. On one hand, both of their air arms acquired French fighters such as the Nieuports and the Morane-Saulnier Nm monoplane. At the same time indigenous fighter designers worked along interestingly divergent paths. While the RFC acquired pushers such as the two-seat Vickers FB 5 Gunbus and Royal Aircraft Factory FE 2b, as well as the single-seat Airco DH 2, to counter the 'Fokker Scourge', the RNAS was getting something more progressive from Thomas O M Sopwith and his chief engineer, Herbert Smith.

The Sopwith scouts' lineage began with the prewar Tabloid racer, a boxy looking but compact single-bay wood and canvas biplane. Although that and a floatplane derivative, christened the Baby, saw service as scouts in the war's early years, Sopwith's first true combat machine was a two-seat reconnaissance-fighter and bomber.

Named for its W-shaped cabane strut arrangement, the 1½ Strutter was passed by the Sopwith experimental department on 12 December 1915. In addition to a Lewis gun for the observer, mounted on an ingenious flexible ring mounting designed by RNAS WO Frederick W Scarff, the aircraft had the first synchronised forward-firing machine gun to be fitted as standard on a British warplane, using Vickers-Challenger interrupter gear. A few weeks after its first test flight, the prototype had the latter gear replaced by an improved system developed by Scarff and Lt Cdr Viktor V Dybovsky, an equally inventive aircraft designer from the Russian Navy who was visiting England at the time. Still later, the 1½ Strutter was fitted with interrupter gear devised by a Flt Sgt Ross, which allowed the pilot to hand-fire his gun if the interrupter mechanism malfunctioned.

In addition to the two-seater, Sopwith produced a single-seat version of the 1½ Strutter, which traded the observer for a heavier bomb load. Both types were issued to 3 Naval Wing, which since serving in the Aegean Sea had been dissolved and re-formed as a strategic bombing unit. On 16 June 1916, the wing arrived at Luxeuil-les-Bains, from where it would join French bomber units in striking at Germany's industrial Saar region – its two-seat 1½ Strutters would escort the single-seat Sopwith bombers.

Commanded by Capt W L Elder, the new 3 Naval Wing formed just as a contingent of Canadian enlistees in the RNAS were graduating from flying school, resulting in an extraordinary percentage being assigned to that unit. Several were destined to become aces.

One Englishman in the unit from whom more would be heard was Flt Cdr Christopher Draper. Born in Liverpool on 15 April 1892, he had earned Royal Aero Club Certificate No 646 on 13 October 1913,

Flt Sub-Lts John E Sharman, H C Lemon and Raymond Collishaw confer in front of a clear-doped Sopwith 1½ Strutter of 3 Naval Wing at Ochey in November 1916 (*Fleet Air Arm Museum JMB/GSL09929*)

joined the RNAS in January 1914 and conducted various armament experiments before being posted to 3 Naval Wing as a flight leader.

After minor bombing attacks combining French and British aircraft, the Luxeuil-based bombers launched their first large-scale effort on 12 October, against the Mauser works at Oberndorf. For this the French fielded 12 Farman F 42 and seven Breguet-Michelin IV pushers, plus a Sopwith 1½ Strutter and Breguet V that were on loan from the British and an escort of four Nieuport 17s from the volunteer *Escadrille Américaine* N 124. The RNAS contributed nine Sopwith 1½ Strutter bombers, six Breguet Vs and seven Sopwith 1½ Strutter fighters.

Most of the bombers reached their objective, where they were engaged by a diverse collection of German fighters (including Ago C Is and Fokker D IIs and D IIIs). No fewer than seven French and three British aeroplanes were shot down. Flt Sub-Lt Raymond Collishaw, a 24-year-old seaman-turned-airman from Nanaimo, British Columbia, piloted Sopwith fighter 9407 with Gunlayer R S Portsmouth in his observer's pit, and he described his experience as follows;

'We left Luxeuil at 1353 hrs in Sopwith B as part of Red Flight. Having stayed with the formation up until we reached enemy lines, I then dropped somewhat behind to close up alongside Butterworth, whose engine seemed to be slowing down. After a few miles Butterworth's engine picked up again and we began to close on the rest of B Flight.

'Five miles beyond the Rhine, on the line of our prepared course, Fleming was attacked by a small machine that had appeared to be engaged with a two-seater enemy machine which carried on below. The small machine that had engaged Fleming closed in and attacked Butterworth, who was abeam my portside. I immediately dived to intercept him, with my engine full on and firing my machine gun. This enemy machine seemed to resemble a Bristol Bullet, painted dark brown without any distinguishing marks as far as I could see. During the dive my engine cut out and I turned around until I was heading towards the Rhine. Butterworth seemed to be still going ahead rather slowly. After losing 2000 ft my engine picked up to 900 revs and I crossed the lines at 6000 ft, at which height I was able to keep afloat at 50 knots.'

While Collishaw struggled with his baulky engine, Flt Sub-Lt Charles H S Butterworth was driven down wounded and taken prisoner by Fokker D II pilot – and future 16-victory ace – Vfw Ludwig Hanstein of *Kampf Einsitzer Kommando* Ensisheim. Flt Lt George R S Fleming escaped his attacker and returned to Luxeuil, however.

Although the British claimed two victories, the Oberndorf raid accomplished little for the losses suffered. Soon afterward, at French request, the wing moved to Ochey, from which it conducted raids into the Saar region north of Nancy.

While ferrying Sopwith 9407 from Luxeuil to Ochey on 25 October – without a gunner, since the route was just behind Allied lines – Collishaw got into some unexpected trouble, as he later reported;

'For some reason I strayed further east than I intended and was jumped by six enemy scouts intent on my destruction. A stream of bullets from one of their number smashed my goggles, filling my eyes with powdered glass. I was hardly able to see and could do little more than fling my machine around in a vain attempt to throw them off. Gradually my sight began to return and I realised that my largely uncontrolled manoeuvring had brought me close to the ground. One of the German machines attempted to come down on me steeply from above, but miscalculated his dive and crashed into a tree.

'With each attack I waited until the enemy was about to open fire then turned inside him. In this way one finally flew across my nose and I sent several bursts into its engine and cockpit. He flipped over and went down vertically – whether he made it down safely or not I don't know.

'Diving into German territory, I shook off my pursuers momentarily, but they caught up with me and I flew deeper into Germany in an effort to shake them off. Finally I did so, and after flying back towards French territory I prepared to land at an aerodrome that I saw below. I put down and taxied in among the aircraft parked on the ground, and then it dawned on me that they bore the German Iron Cross marking! I jammed the throttle forward and managed to take off, although I clipped the tops off two trees close to the field.'

The two German aeroplanes were credited to Collishaw as his first victories. They would not be the last.

On 9, 10 and 11 November 3 Naval Wing attacked the iron works and blast furnaces at Volkingen. Draper was flying Sopwith 1½ Strutter 9407, with Flt Sub-Lt L V Pearkes as his gunner, on the 10th, leading seven other fighters to protect ten Sopwith bombers. During the mission, Draper reported that 'a Fokker approached from behind and the passenger fired half a tray. I turned immediately and opened fire, before diving, turning and climbing once again. This caused the enemy pilot to turn across my bows. I opened fire, following him round until he suddenly dived. The aircraft was observed spinning to earth'.

Sopwith 1½ Strutter N5098 was an example of the single-seat bombers that the two-seaters were meant to escort on missions. The fuselage numbers were a later supplement to the geometric figures that identified individual aeroplanes within 'Blue' and 'Red' flights of 3 Naval Wing (*Fleet Air Arm Museum JMB/GSL06008*)

Soon afterward, Draper added to his report;

'Sighted two enemy biplanes. These machines were engaged by turning quickly and meeting them end on. After manoeuvring and fighting continuously for about ten minutes, one was driven off and the other hung onto our tail. It is probable that his gun jammed, as he approached close in without firing. Sub Lt Pearkes fired a whole tray at him and he was seen to nosedive to earth.'

Draper and Pearkes were jointly credited with both enemy aircraft. While leading a three-aeroplane line patrol on 23 November, Draper and Flt Sub-Lt Barker, in Sopwith 9722, encountered two enemy machines and brought one of them down. Its demise was witnessed by French ground observers. The next day nine bombers set out for the blast furnaces at Dillingen, with Draper and Barker (again in 9407) leading seven fighters as escorts. Ft Lt C B Dalinson, flying Sopwith 9739 with Sub-Lt F E Fraser, reported;

'Two enemy aircraft attacked No 16, Flt Cdr Draper, and myself in turn. My Gunlayer, Sub-Lt Fraser, emptied a tray-and-a-half into one machine, but the other left the fight. The first machine was then tackled by No 16, and he finally dived straight at me. I stalled slightly to get my front gun at him, and was able to fire 100 rounds or so right into his engine and fuselage from point blank. An explosive bullet hit the centre section, a splinter hitting the tip of my leg. He passed a few feet above my top plane and then wavered, spun and dived, and I observed him fall to bits in the air before hitting the ground over a wood northeast of Delmo.'

Jointly credited to the two crews, this latest success brought Draper's tally to four.

The high attrition rate suffered by RFC units in early 1917 led Gen Sir Douglas Haig and Maj Gen Trenchard to request the transfer of RNAS units to RFC control. They also judged 3 Naval Wing's long-distance bombing campaign to be an insufficiently productive diversion of aircraft and aircrews from more vital air operations.

At the end of January the first nine pilots left 3 Naval Wing to form the nucleus of a new fighter unit, 3 Naval Squadron. Among them were Canadians Ray Collishaw, Joseph S T Fall, James A Glen, John J Malone and Arthur T Whealy. Subsequent transferees destined for acedom included William Melville Alexander, George B Anderson, Frederick C Armstrong, Alfred W Carter, William H Chisam, Desmond F Fitzgibbon, John A Page, Ellis V Reid and John E Sharman. A week after flying its 18th, and final, raid (Freiburg on 14 April 1917), 3 Naval Wing parcelled out its remaining aircrewmen and bequeathed the last of its Sopwith 1½ Strutters to the French.

Sopwith 1½ Strutter 9722, while crewed by Flt Lt John D Newberry and PO Rees, came to the aid of single-seat bomber N5088, flown by Flt Sub-Lt Ambrose B Shearer, which was under attack by a German two-seater on 10 November 1916. Newberry and Rees succeeded in driving the enemy machine down, the aircraft being seen to sideslip into the woods below (*Fleet Air Arm Museum JMB/GSL06006*)

SINGLE-SEAT SOPWITHS

Soon after the 1½ Strutter entered production, it was joined by a smaller, single-seat derivative armed with a single Vickers. Cleared for testing on 9 February 1916, the aircraft made an immediate impression on everyone who flew it. Fitted with a Le Rhône engine that produced a mere 80 hp, the single-seater could nevertheless attain a speed of 110 mph at 6500 ft and climb to 10,000 ft in 12 minutes. Moreover, it combined docile handling, sprightly manoeuvrability and good cockpit visibility in one of the war's most aesthetically pleasing airframes.

The RNAS ordered the Scout, as it was officially called, in April, by which time Sopwith's Australian-born foreman of works, Henry A Kauper, had developed an improved synchronising mechanism over the Scarff-Dybovsky sytem. When Maj Gen Trenchard read a copy of the Admiralty's report on the aeroplane's performance, he pencilled in the margin, 'Let's get a squadron of these'. Another RFC officer, Col Sefton Brancker, allegedly remarked upon seeing a Scout alongside its forebear, 'Good God! Your 1½ Strutter has had a pup'. In spite of official efforts to discourage it, the new fighter became universally known by that name.

By the time the first Pups had reached 'A' Naval Squadron of 1 Naval Wing at Dunkirk in July 1916, the prototype of another variant was joining them for evaluation. Completed on 30 May 1916, Sopwith Triplane N500 combined the Pup's fuselage with three sets of narrow-chord, high aspect ratio wings that gave the pilot a better view from the cockpit and superior manoeuvrability even to the Pup's. The fighter was powered by a 130 hp Clerget engine that endowed it with a top speed of 120 mph, a rate-of-climb of 10,000 ft in 12 minutes and a 20,000 ft ceiling.

Flying the new 'Triplehound', Flt Lt R S Dallas drove a two-seater down OOC on 1 July, followed by a scout OOC on 30 September. Again duly impressed, the Admiralty ordered the Triplane into production. Oddly enough, the first confirmed Pup victory had been scored just six days before Dallas' *second* Triplane success. On 24 September Flt Sub-Lt Stan Goble used prototype Pup 3691 to down an LVG OOC over Ghistelles for his third victory.

On the 25th Flt Sub-Lt Edward Rochfort Grange, in Pup N5182, scored the type's second success. Born on 11 January 1892 in Lansing, Michigan, where his Canadian parents ran a veterinary college, 'Roch' Grange lived in Toronto from 1908. When war broke out he returned to the United States to train at the Curtiss Flying School, graduating on 20 September 1915 and subsequently joining 1 Naval Wing in February 1916.

'My first confirmed victory was a large seaplane shot down in the sea about five miles off the coast at Ostend', Grange recalled. 'I saw Mulock and gave the story verbally to him, and he in turn relayed the location to our Royal Navy who picked up the remains and brought them to St Pol aerodrome, Dunkirk. The French gave me the *Croix de Guerre*'.

Grange's victim was a Sablatnig SF 2 of *Seeflugstaffel* I. The crewmen, Ltn zur Sees Otto Soltenborn and Hans Röthig, were killed.

On 22 October Galbraith destroyed a floatplane off Blankenberghe, but generally the Sopwith pilots at Dunkirk were finding little action. Events over the Somme were to change all that, with Trenchard's appeal for RNAS reinforcements leading to the formation of 8 Naval Squadron from flights drawn from 1, 4 and 5 Naval Wings. All of its pilots were volunteers and, given the relatively idle time they had been having in Flanders, they were enthusiastic ones, including Murray Galbraith, Stan Goble and 'Roch' Grange. Organised at St Pol-sur-Mer on 26 October, 'Naval 8' was despatched south to relieve No 32 Sqn RFC at Vert Galand. There, it came under the command of No 22 Wing, 5th Brigade, and commenced operations on 3 November.

First blood was drawn on 10 November when Flt Sub-Lt Stanley V Trapp forced a scout to land and Galbraith sent another down OOC. Six days later Goble and Galbraith each claimed an LVG OOC. On the 23rd Galbraith attacked six LVGs, shooting down one and forcing three others to land. Credited with the one destroyed for his sixth victory, he was awarded a Bar to his DSC and the French CdG. At that point, however, Galbraith's nerves gave out, and after being withdrawn to rest

With two previous victories in Nieuports, Australian Flt Sub-Lt Stanley James Goble of 'A' Naval Squadron, 1 Naval Wing, scored the first Sopwith Pup victory when he sent an LVG down OOC near Ghistelles on 24 September 1916 while flying the prototype 3691. Later, serving with 'Naval 8', Goble claimed five more victories in Pup N5194 (*Norman Franks*)

Like Goble, Canadian Flt Sub-Lt Daniel Murray Bayne Galbraith had scored two victories in Nieuports while with 'A' Naval Squadron, 1 Naval Wing, before using a Pup to down a floatplane on 22 October 1916. He later claimed three more victories while flying Pups with 'Naval 8' (*Greg VanWyngarden*)

On 23 November 1916, Flt Lt Robert Alexander Little destroyed a two-seater from FA (A) 221 in flames northeast of La Bassée. He would score thrice more in Pups with 'Naval 8' before going on an aerial rampage in Triplanes (*Jon Guttman*)

Reginald Rhys Soar, shown at right with 'Naval 8' squadronmate H L Huskinson, claimed two Halberstadts on 20 December 1916 while flying Pup N5181. He went on to add ten more to his score in Triplanes by 27 July 1917 (*N Franks*)

on 1 December, he served as an instructor and flew anti-submarine patrols over the Adriatic. Galbraith joined the RCAF after the war, but was killed in a car accident on 29 March 1921.

Also on 23 November, Australian Flt Lt Robert Alexander Little destroyed a spotter aeroplane from *Flieger Abteilung* (*Artillerie*) (FA (A)) 221 in flames northeast of La Bassée, killing Vfw Friedrich Schwalm and Oblt Johann Köln. Born in Melbourne on 19 July 1895, Bob Little was the son of a businessman who sold medical and surgical equipment. His family had emigrated from Scotland to Canada, before moving on to Australia. Educated at Scotch College, Melbourne, he travelled to England when war broke out and trained at his own expense to gain his flying certificate on 27 October 1915, after which he joined the RNAS. In January 1916 Little was posted to Eastchurch, and by late June he was in Dunkirk flying Bristol Scouts and 1½ Strutters. He would subsequently join 'Naval 8'.

On 4 December Little drove down a Halberstadt D II OOC, while Flt Sub-Lt George Goodman Simpson, a 20-year-old Australian from St Kilda, Melbourne, with previous experience in 1 Naval Wing, sent an Albatros D I down OOC northeast of Bapaume. On the 20th Little added a two-seater to his score, while squadronmate Flt Sub-Lt Reginald Rhys Soar downed two Halberstadts. Born on 24 August 1893, 'Reggie' Soar had joined the RNAS on 10 August 1915 and flown bombing missions in 1½ Strutters with 5 Naval Wing prior to joining 'Naval 8'. The squadron would continue to make a name for itself over the sector until eventually relieved by another Pup unit, 3 Naval Squadron, in February 1917.

Another of 'Naval 8's' future paladins, Flt Sub-Lt Robert John Orton Compston, was flying Nieuport 8750 when he opened his account on 26 December with an Albatros two-seater OOC north of Cambrai. Born on 9 January 1898, Compston was a vicar's son who joined the RNAS in August 1915 and served in home defence prior to being posted to 'Naval 8'. By the end of the month Pups had replaced the last of the squadron's Nieuports.

On 4 January 1917, Grange was leading Little and Flt Sub-Lt Allan S Todd when they dived on seven Albatros D IIs. Grange claimed an enemy aircraft destroyed and two OOC, but three Albatros scouts got on Todd's tail. Little, coming to his assistance, saw Todd twist to the left and lose his left wings. As both sides retired, Little observed a crowd gathered around Todd's Pup, while a German aeroplane lay on its back nearby and two others had force landed in the adjacent field.

Grange got credit for all three claims, although his *Jasta* 'Boelcke' opponents suffered no casualties. Todd had been slain by Ltn Manfred *Freiherr* von Richthofen, who cut serial N5187 from the fighter's fuselage for his trophy collection and submitted his own report of the action;

'About 1615 hrs, just starting out, we saw above us at 4000 metres altitude four aeroplanes, unmolested

Flt Sub-Lt Charles Dawson Booker opened his account with 'Naval 8' in Pup N5197 on 23 January 1917 when he sent an Albatros D III down OOC – this aircraft may have been from *Jasta* 'Boelcke'. He came fully into his stride in Sopwith Triplanes, however, claiming four victories during 'Bloody April' and another nine in May. Booker's total of 29 included wounding Oblt Adolf *Ritter* von Tutschek, commander of *Jasta* 12. On 13 August 1918 he was killed by another *Jasta* 12 pilot, Ltn Ulrich Neckel (*Norman Franks*)

by our artillery. Only when they were approaching did we notice they were English. One of the English aeroplanes attacked us, and we saw immediately that the enemy aeroplane was superior to ours. Only because we were three against one did we detect the enemy's weak points. I managed to get behind him and shot him down. The aeroplane broke apart whilst falling.'

Grange, Little and Flt Sub-Lt A H S Lawson were conducting a patrol with No 32 Sqn on 7 January when the latter's DH 2s were jumped over Beugny by four *Jasta* 'Boelcke' Albatros D IIs led by Ltn Erwin Böhme, who killed 2Lt E S Wagner of the RFC. Little's engine was only producing 800 rpm and he was about to turn for home when he noticed an Albatros diving behind a BE 2. Giving chase, he fired 60 rounds at 100 yards and saw the D II nose-dive over Grevillers. After fending off attacks by two other Albatrosen, he returned to have his fourth victory confirmed. Grange was also credited with an Albatros OOC for his fifth, but was wounded in the right shoulder. Although faint from blood loss, he made Allied lines and after recovery spent the rest of the war as an instructor. Attending the last international aces' reunion in Paris in 1981, Grange died in Toronto on 13 July 1988.

On 23 January, Flt Lt Charles Dawson Booker downed an Albatros D II OOC northeast of Bapaume. Born in Speldhurst, Kent, on 21 April 1897, Booker spent most of his youth in Australia before returning to England with his parents in 1911. On 8 September 1915 he joined the RNAS and served with 5 Naval Wing from May 1916 to 26 October, when he transferred to 'Naval 8'.

On 1 February, 3 Naval Squadron arrived to take 'Naval 8's' place while it re-equipped with Triplanes at St Pol. 'At Vert Galand, we took over old Sopwith Pups from 8 Naval Squadron, and they certainly had had a bashing before we got them', recalled Edmund Pierce. Born in England to a Quaker family on 22 October 1893, he had served in the Friends' Ambulance Unit in France, but decided to join the RNAS in June 1916. After being declared 'ready for active service' on 27 December, Pierce was posted to 'Naval 3'. 'I was assigned to "C" Flight under Flt Lt R G Mack', he noted, 'with Flt Sub-Lts R Collishaw, F C Armstrong, A T Whealy and L H Rochford completing the six. I did not realise then in what distinguished company I was flying'.

One of Pierces' flightmates, Flt Sub-Lt Leonard Henry Rochford, was born in Enfield on 10 November 1896 and, being too young to be accepted in the RNAS when war was declared, learned to fly with the London Provincial Flying Club at Hendon before enlisting in May 1916. After a time with the War Flight at Eastchurch, he joined 3 Naval Squadron on 24 January 1917 and was assigned to 'C' Flight under Flt Lt Robin G Mack.

The latter pilot opened 'Naval 3's' account over the Somme with a two-seater on 14 February, which Collishaw duly followed up with a Halberstadt D II OOC the next day. On the 28th the unit relocated to Bertangles.

Escorting two Morane-Saulnier Parasols of No 3 Sqn RFC on 5 March, Mack and Rochford were attacked by five Albatros scouts over Manoncourt. 'They were very close and just above me', wrote Rochford. 'I heard the rat-tat-tat of their Spandau guns and felt frightened as I

Flying Pups with 'Naval 3', Flt Sub-Lt Leonard Henry Rochford claimed his first victory on 4 March 1917 when he sent an Albatros D I OOC. Downing a seaplane for his third success on 7 July, he came fully into his own in Camels and ultimately became his squadron's leading ace with 29 victories. Finding employment as an engineer postwar, 'Titch' Rochford also wrote an excellent memoir, *I Chose the Sky* (*Mike Westrop*)

manoeuvred my Pup to prevent one getting his sights on me. Suddenly a mottled brown and black Albatros dived from the right, in front of me, to attack Mack. Quickly, I fired a burst at him. He fell away sideways and I lost sight of him as I looked for the other enemy aircraft. They had broken off the fight and were diving steeply away eastwards'.

Rochford was 'very pleased' when Mack confirmed an 'Albatros D I' OOC for his first victory, but two other flights of 'Naval 3' Pups, escorting FE 2bs of No 18 Sqn over Cambrai, had a bigger scrap with Halberstadt D IIs of *Jasta* 1 with more mixed results. Four enemy aircraft were credited, including one each to Collishaw and Malone, but *Jasta* 1 recorded no casualties, whereas Ltn Herbert Schröder and Oblt Hans Kummetz killed Flt Lt Henry R Wambolt and Flt Sub-Lt J P White, and a badly wounded Flt Sub-Lt L A Powell crashed in Allied lines and subsequently died in hospital three days later.

'Naval 3's' next successes came on 11 March when 23-year-old Australian Flt Cdr Bertram Charles Bell and Flt Lt Herbert Gardner Travers of A Flight claimed a two-seater each OOC over Bapaume. Born on 1 April 1891, 'Tiny' Travers had been a machine gunner with the Honourable Artillery Company before transferring to the RNAS on 14 December 1915, and joining 1 Naval Wing on 27 May 1916. After rest leave in England, he returned to the front with 'Naval 3'.

'It was about the middle of the month of March that another bunch of Canadians joined us from 3 Naval Wing', Rochford wrote, 'among them Flt Sub-Lt A W Carter of Calgary, Alberta, who was always known to us as "Nick"'. Born in Fish Creek on 29 April 1894, Alfred William Carter had enlisted in the 46th Queen's University Battery before applying for flight training in 1915. Discharged from the army, he trained in Florida prior to joining the RNAS on 23 May 1916. Carter served in 3 Naval Wing from 15 November to 7 March, when he was reassigned. '"B" Flight, "3 Naval" were a good lot', Carter remarked. 'Flt Cdr T C Vernon was our flight CO'.

'During the morning of 17 March', Rochford stated, 'our three flights carried out an operation to clear the sky of enemy aircraft on the 5th Army front so that FEs of No 18 Sqn, RFC could carry out a reconnaissance. This could be called an Offensive Sweep and Escort combined. "A" Flight patrolled at the lowest altitude and just above the FEs, "B" Flight flew above "A" Flight and "C" Flight was stacked above them at 17,000 ft'.

The Pups had a succession of engagements, during which 'A' Flight's Flt Lt Bell claimed an Albatros in flames and 26-year-old Irish Flt Sub-Lt Francis Dominic Casey, a former observer with 2 Naval Wing who had since taken pilot training, downed one OOC. The most aggressive Pup pilot that day, Flt Sub-Lt John Joseph Malone, was credited with a two-seater OOC and two Albatros D IIs in flames. Although born in the United States on 20 December 1894, 'Jack' Malone's parents were Canadian, and when war broke out he enlisted in the RNAS, serving in 3 Naval Wing and then 'Naval 3'.

Collishaw left at the end of March when his face became swollen with frostbite, and in April he would be re-posted to newly forming 10 Naval Squadron. Meanwhile, on the 28th, 'Naval 3' moved to Marieux aerodrome.

THE TRIPLANE TREND

The savaging of British aircraft during the Arras offensive known as 'Bloody April' brought two fighters in particular to the public eye. Certainly the Albatros D III and the *Jastas* equipped with it were at the top of their game, dominating the sky and contributing primarily to the loss of three British aeroplanes for every German. In that same month, however, the Sopwith Triplane began to assert itself – sufficiently to affect German fighter design as much as the Nieuport sesquiplanes had in 1916.

In the wake of Stan Dallas' successes with the Triplane in the latter half of 1916, '1 Naval' was fully equipped with the aircraft. Dallas flew N5436 when he downed an LVG on 1 February. Later that month the unit moved from Dunkirk to Chipilly, south of Albert and east of Amiens. First blood in the sector was drawn on 5 April, again by Dallas in N5436, with an Albatros D II OOC.

Triplane-equipped 'Naval 8' returned to the Somme sector at Auchel in March, followed by a move to St-Eloi, northwest of Arras. Scoring resumed on 5 April when Flt Sub-Lt Compston downed a Halberstadt D II OOC southeast of La Bassée. Dallas claimed an Albatros two-seater the following day, as did 20-year-old Flt Sub-Lt Thomas Grey Culling from Auckland, New Zealand, and Flt Sub-Lt B Clayton. Three Canadian aces of 'Naval 3' also made their debuts that day, as 22-year-old Flt Lt Lloyd Samuel Breadner from Carlton Place, Ontario, and 21-year-old Flt Sub-Lt Joseph Stewart Temple Fall from Millbank, British Columbia, destroyed Halberstadt D IIs while escorting BE 2cs over the Bois de Bourlon, and Nick Carter got another OOC.

On the 7th Bob Little of 'Naval 8' took on two Albatros D IIIs and sent one spiralling down to crash northeast of Arras. It was Little's fifth victory overall and his first in a Triplane (he was flying N5469). Booker of 'Naval 1' downed an Albatros D II OOC near Lens that evening. The following day 20-year-old Flt Lt Anthony Rex Arnold from Fareham, Hampshire, opened his account with 'Naval 8' with an Albatros D III OOC near Beaumont. Pup pilots Travers and Casey of 'Naval 3' also claimed D IIIs OOC that afternoon. The Battle of Arras officially began on 9 April, and that day Little claimed a Halberstadt OOC.

'Naval 3' had what 'Titch' Rochford called 'a notable day' on 11 April when 'B' Flight escorted BE 2cs of No 4 Sqn RFC on a bombing mission to Cambrai. En route to the target Breadner, in Pup N6181, downed a two-seater in flames at 0845 hrs. Ten minutes later the BEs were assailed by Albatros and Halberstadt scouts of *Jasta* 12, two falling victim to Ltns Georg Röth and Adolf Schulte. Breadner drove an Albatros down OOC and sent another spinning earthward – a wing was seen to break off the latter machine. Flt Sub-Lt P G McNeill also claimed an OOC.

Born in Fareham, Hampshire, on 26 August 1896, Flt Sub-Lt Anthony Rex Arnold of 'Naval 8' scored three of his five victories during 'Bloody April' 1917. He later rose to the rank of major and was given command of No 79 Sqn RAF (*Norman Franks*)

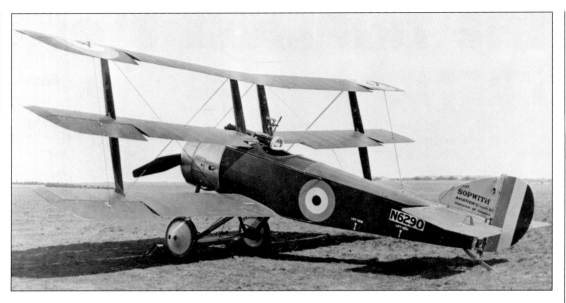

Triplane N6290, which was later named *DIXIE*, was flown by ace A R Arnold during its service with 'Naval 8'. He scored his fourth and fifth victories while flying this machine in the early summer of 1917 (*Bruce/Leslie*)

Joe Fall, in N6158, despatched an Albatros D II in flames and duelled three others down to 200 ft before shooting one opponent in the head, after which the Albatros spun to the ground and the others disengaged. Five minutes later, Fall was attacked by a Halberstadt, which he looped over, fired at and sent crashing to earth. Crossing the lines under intense ground fire, Fall landed his bullet-riddled Pup at No 35 Sqn's aerodrome. Squadronmate Flt Sub-Lt S Bennett also returned with a shot-up Pup, N5199 being declared fit only for scrapping.

A fighting debut of a different sort befell 21-year-old South African Flt Sub-Lt Edwin Tufnell Hayne of 'A' Flight. Shot down by Ltn Schulte, Hayne emerged in a state of shock but was otherwise unhurt and, doubly fortunate, had come down in Allied lines. He would later achieve acedom in Sopwith Camels.

Flt Cdr Mack led 'Naval 3's' 'B' Flight as it escorted No 18 Sqn on 12 April when *Jasta* 12 attacked them over Pronville. Twenty-year-old Flt Sub-Lt Frederick Carr Armstrong from Toronto shared credit for

Flt Sub-Lt Joseph S T Fall poses beside Pup N6181 *HMA HAPPY*, in which Flt Lt Lloyd Breadner scored five of his seven Pup victories in the spring of 1917. Fall claimed the first of his 36 credited victories in N6158 when he destroyed a Halberstadt D II over Bourlon Wood on 6 April, while Breadner, in N5199, got another for his first (*Norman Franks*)

an Albatros OOC with Pierce, who claimed a second OOC, while another of the unit's Canadians, 23-year-old Flt Sub-Lt Arthur Treloar Whealy, was credited with a third. Mack was believed to have despatched an opponent that was seen to shed its wings, but he was in turn wounded and brought down at Marquin by *Jasta* 12's CO, Hptm Paul Hennig von Osterroht. Mack's Pup, N6172 *Black Tulip*, was captured intact, and he had to have his foot amputated. Mack's perceived victim was probably Ltn Schulte, who had collided with FE 2b 4995 moments before. This was the only German casualty in spite of No 18 Sqn claiming two for the loss of two 'Fees', the second falling to Vfw Arthur Schörisch.

'Naval 1's' Teddy Gerrard resumed his scoring in Triplane N5440 at 0820 hrs on 14 April with an enemy aeroplane OOC over Epinoy. 'Naval 8's' Triplanes returned to the fray 30 minutes later as Flt Lt Booker led a 'C' Flight patrol, during which he downed an LVG OOC. Twenty-year-old Flt Sub-Lt Edward Duncan Crundall, who had been in the RNAS since 1914, fell behind with a missing engine and was attacked by two Albatros two-seaters. 'I literally saw red and dived on the tail of the nearest, firing my gun all the time', Crundall recounted. The enemy aircraft went into a steep nosedive, but Crundall's elation was rudely jarred by the other German's gunfire. He then attacked that Albatros too, diving after it until he realised his wings were in danger of coming off. Easing out of the dive, Crundall nursed his aeroplane back against the west wind, requiring 30 minutes to reach the first Allied aerodrome. He was credited with both enemy aircraft destroyed.

'Naval 8' covered an FE 2b patrol of No 25 Sqn RFC on the 21st, and when the latter came under attack by Albatros D IIIs of *Jasta* 30, Little came down and engaged one from a distance of just 20 yards. The German, apparently Ltn Oskar Seitz, was caught between Little and the FE observer he was attacking, and after nearly colliding with his intended victim, went down to crash land northeast of Oppy, emerging unhurt. Suffering a gun jam, Little accompanied the stricken FE as it glided to a crash landing near Bouvigny Wood, then alit nearby to see to the crew, who turned out to be uninjured.

In the same action Flt Lt Arnold claimed an Albatros in flames and then combined his gunfire with that of Lt R G Malcolm and 2Lt J B Weir of No 25 Sqn to send another crashing at Thelus-Vitry before his gun jammed. The latter, Albatros D III 2147/16, was given the British captured aircraft serial G22, its pilot, Ltn Gustav Nernst, being killed.

'Naval 3' topped 21 April off with two Albatros D IIIs driven down OOC by Casey, and one each by Travers, Malone and Flt Sub-Lt Hubert S Broad. 'Naval 1's' Dallas claimed four victories between the 22nd and 24th, while Culling got two.

Those three days also saw 'Naval 3's' Pups equally as busy. On 22 April Pierce downed a D III, while Flt Sub-Lt Harold Spencer Kerby got a two-seater OOC for his second victory. Born in Calgary, Alberta, on 14 May 1893, and earning his flying certificate at the Graham White School at Hendon in May 1915, Kerby had served with 3 Naval Wing in the Dardanelles and then with 'Naval 9' when it was based near Dunkirk. Whilst serving with the latter unit he had shared in the destruction of a German floatplane on 24 March 1917.

Thomas F N Gerrard scored his first victory in a Nieuport with 'A' Naval Squadron of 1 Naval Wing on 8 July 1916, and went on to claim seven more in Triplanes with 'Naval 1' – six of them in N5440. His tenth success came in a Camel on 6 April 1918, shared with squadronmates as a major in No 208 Sqn RAF (*Mike Westrop*)

The action on St George's Day (23 April) started at 0630 hrs with 20-year-old Flt Sub-Lt Harold Francis Beamish from Havelock North, New Zealand, opening his account with an Albatros D III OOC, as did Ottawa-born Flt Sub-Lt George Benson Anderson with a D II OOC. Pierce and Kerby also scored. 'However, it was Jack Malone on his own who had the most fun', Rochford recalled. 'He engaged an enemy aircraft, shot the pilot and the aeroplane crashed. He then drove a second enemy aircraft down out of control before attacking a third. Running out of ammunition, he landed at an RFC aerodrome to replenish, took off again and recrossed the lines, where he drove down two more enemy aircraft out of control before returning to Marieux'.

At 1000 hrs a twin-engined Gotha bomber was spotted over Marieux. Several Pups scrambled, but it was Breadner who caught up with the enemy. 'I saw a hostile aircraft over Marieux and proceeded at once in pursuit', he reported. 'On reaching the hostile aircraft's height of 12,000 ft, I closed in on its tail and opened fire at a range of 50 yards. I fired about 100 rounds and then my gun jammed. However, I had hit its engines and was able to force the pilot to land in a field southeast of Vron, where the machine went up on its nose. I landed close by and walked to the machine and found three men already under arrest – the pilot and two observers. All of its bombs had exploded bar one'.

Breadner, who returned to Marieux with the German pilot's flying helmet and other souvenirs including crosses cut from the fuselage fabric, claimed that his victim had been on a test flight when it blundered over 'Naval 3's' aerodrome. After partially burning their machine Offz Stv Alfred Heidner and Ltns Kurt Karl Josef Scheuren and Otto Wirth from *Kampfstaffel* 15 of *Kagohl (Kampfgeschwader der Obersten der Heeresleitung)* 3 became prisoners.

The 23rd climaxed for 'Naval 3' at 1730 hrs when *Jastas* 12 and 33 attacked FE 2bs of No 18 Sqn over Baralle and the Pups rushed

Flt Sub-Lt Alexander McDonald Shook stands at left with his Pup N6200 *Bobs* at Bray Dunes, with Flt Sub-Lt Geoffrey M Hemming at right (the two pilots in the middle remain unidentified). Shook scored 'Naval 4's' first victory in N6200 on 24 April 1917, and he added two more in the same aeroplane before engine failure forced him to ditch it in the sea on 19 May. Recovered, N6200 continued to serve in Home Defence until it was struck off charge in March 1918, having endured several more crashes by then (*Norman Franks*)

to their aid. The FEs claimed four assailants, and eight more were credited to 'Naval 3', including one D III destroyed and one OOC by Carter, one destroyed by Kerby and an OOC each for Casey, Whealy, Breadner and Fall, the latter two 'making ace' in the process. Among the 'destroyed' were two genuine German casualties, Uffz Nauczak of *Jasta* 33, who was severely wounded over Quéant, and *Jasta* 12's CO, Hptm von Osterroht, who was killed near Cambrai.

On 24 April a new ace and a new scout unit made their debuts. Born in Tioga, Ontario, on 2 December 1888, Flt Lt Alexander MacDonald Shook had flown 1½ Strutters with 5 Naval Wing until its 'A' Naval Squadron was reorganised as 4 Naval Squadron, based at Bray Dunes. Flying Pup N6200, he drove a 'Fokker D II' down OOC over Ghistelles for his first of 12 victories.

On the Somme Front that morning, two Albatros D IIIs were credited as OOC to Gerrard of 'Naval 1'. George Simpson and Bob Little of 'Naval 8' each claimed a D III OOC, but Ltn Heinrich Gontermann of *Jasta* 5 killed one of their squadronmates, Flt Sub-Lt E B J Walter. Booker drove a two-seater down near Douai with its observer hit and the aircraft trailing smoke, but judging it still to be under control, he did submit a claim.

Around noon Little departed Vert Galand in response to reports of an approaching enemy aircraft, and he duly spotted a two-seater 12,000 ft above Auchel aerodrome. As he dived, he saw two Nieuport 17s from No 40 Sqn RFC, flown by Lt Ian P R Napier and J A G Brewis, also descending on the German. 'He turned north and I followed, firing whenever the opportunity presented itself', Little reported. 'I noticed that the observer was not returning my fire so I closed in on him. He was losing height all the time, and when a mile east of Bethune I observed my tracers going into his fuselage. I was then firing from a range of 10 to 15 yards. He then nosedived and I dived after him. He landed in a field and I was unable to get my engine to start after the dive and had to land alongside the hostile machine. I ran into a ditch and overturned. I got out of the machine and went across to the Germans and took them prisoner. The pilot told me he knew he would never get back when he saw me coming to attack him'.

The DFW C V, from FA (*Luftbild*) 18, had landed northeast of Oppy. Given captured aircraft serial G24, it was jointly credited to Napier, Brewis and Little. The latter invited his captives, Ltns Hans Huppertz and Friedrich Neumüller, to 'Naval 8's' aerodrome, where Crundall later described the visit;

'The three of them went to lunch and soon they were the best

Robert Little scored 20 of his 24 Triplane victories with 'Naval 8' in N5493 between 28 April and 10 July 1917. The second most successful Triplane in aerial combat after Ray Collishaw's N5492, *BLYMP* was badly shot up in combat on 28 July while being flown by future ace E D Crundall. Having been repaired, N5493 was eventually destroyed in a mid-air collision with a SPAD VII from No 19 Sqn RAF on 6 September 1917 (*Philip Jarrett*)

of pals, exchanging souvenirs and relating their various experiences. The Germans spoke good English, and both of them had been awarded the Iron Cross. They were very surprised when large plates of meat were served to them because, in Germany, they said, meat was very scarce.'

After the war Neumüller tried to contact Little and, upon learning he had died, wrote to his widow;

'Because he was so amiable to me on the darkest day of my soldier's life, I will never forget him. He was in every respect a knightly adversary of the air.'

Neumüller sent Mrs Little a Christmas card every year thereafter except during World War 2.

At 1650 hrs on 24 April, Travers led 'Naval 3's' 'A' Flight in an attack on a two-seater near Morchies. After firing bursts at close range, Travers and Casey disengaged with jammed guns. Lagging due to a faulty engine, Malone had put the sun at his back before joining in, and reported;

'I was then in a good position to attack, and after a burst of fire the rear gunner (Observer) dropped down into his cockpit but soon came up again and fired at me when I had closed to about 20 yards range. He then disappeared again into his cockpit. I forced the enemy aircraft to land intact. I then opened my throttle but my engine refused to respond. So, I landed beside the enemy aircraft and we were shelled by German artillery after helping the German pilot to remove the badly wounded observer from his cockpit. He died within ten minutes. The German pilot was slightly wounded in the head. He said he did not see me approach to attack out of the sun and he thought he was landing behind his own lines.'

Both DFW C V 5927/16 and Malone's Pup, N6208, were demolished. The former, whose remains were given the captured designation G25, was jointly credited to Casey, Malone and Travers, earning the latter acedom and, in June, the DSC. Although the German observer, Ltn Karl Keim of FA 26, had died, for a few days 'Naval 3' held the pilot, Uffz Max Haase, in its officers' mess. '"Tiny" Travers was detailed to look after him and to get from him all possible useful information', Rochford wrote. 'He was a pleasant, friendly little man with a sense of humour. He was also something of an artist and drew several pencil sketches for us. I remember one of them was of a very full-breasted woman under which he wrote in German the caption "Double-Seater". On his departure he said he had enjoyed staying with us very much'.

Another future Canadian ace of 'Naval 4' opened his account with an Albatros D II OOC on 26 April. Born in Toronto on 23 August 1896, Flt Sub-Lt Arnold Jaques Chadwick had flown 1½ Strutters with 5 Naval Wing and was shot down while bombing Zeppelin sheds on 2 October 1916, evading capture to reach neutral Holland and eventually be repatriated. Booker of 'Naval 8' downed a D III on the 26th, as did 'Naval 3's' Casey and Malone.

On 28 April Bob Little downed a two-seater over Oppy. That evening, during a patrol along the Flanders coast, new Triplane unit 'Naval 10', based at Furnes, opened its account when an Albatros D II was shot down over Ostend. The victory fell to Raymond Collishaw, recovered from frostbite and reassigned to lead the unit's 'B' Flight.

Flt Lt Herbert G Travers of 'Naval 3' claimed his fifth victory on 24 April 1917 when he shared in the destruction of DFW C V 5927/16 of FA 26, killing the observer, Ltn Karl Keim, and wounding the pilot, Uffz Max Haase, who for a few days was entertained at the officers' mess. '"Tiny" Travers was detailed to look after him, and to get from him all possible useful information', Len Rochford recalled. 'On his departure he said he had enjoyed staying with us very much' (*Norman Franks*)

The following day Fall, Casey, Breadner, Broad and Carter of 'Naval 3' each added an Albatros D III to their scores, but otherwise the Triplanes dominated the day. Flt Cdr Gerrard of 'Naval 1' was credited with a D III OOC and 19-year-old Australian Flt Sub-Lt Richard Pearman Minifie from Melbourne destroyed another. Flt Sub-Lt Cyril Burfield Ridley, an Englishman by birth living in Toronto when war broke out, and Herbert Victor Rowley shared in the downing of a two-seater OOC. Later that afternoon Flt Sub-Lt A P Heywood claimed an Albatros D II destroyed.

During the evening of 29 April 1 and 8 Naval Squadrons took on the 'Red Baron's' best over their home turf. Earlier that day Hptm Manfred von Richthofen, in his all-red Albatros D III, and his command, *Jasta* 11, were in peak form as the baron, his brother Lothar and Ltn Kurt Wolff each shot down a SPAD VII, after which von Richthofen and Wolff downed FE 2bs and the latter destroyed a BE 2f.

At 1925 hrs the brothers von Richthofen added a BE 2e to each of their scores. Soon after that, *Jasta* 11 encountered what Manfred reported as 'a strong enemy one-seater force of Nieuports, SPADs and Triplanes'. Both 1 and 8 Naval Squadrons had machines up at that time, and it seems to have been six of the latter, with Flt Cdr Arnold leading Flt Sub-Lts Little, A R Knight, Philip A Johnston, Roderick McDonald and Albert Edward Cuzner, that first engaged the Germans between Fresnoy and Gavrelle.

'We flew on', von Richthofen later wrote, 'climbing to higher altitude, for above us some of the "Anti-Richthofen Club" had gathered together. Again, we were easy to recognise, the sun from the west illuminating the aircraft and letting their beautiful red colour be seen from far away. We closed up tightly, for each of us knew we were dealing with "brothers" who pursued the same trade we did. Unfortunately, they were higher than we were, so we had to wait for their attack. The famous Triplanes and SPADs were new machines, but it is not a matter of the crate as much as who sits in it – the "brothers" were wary and had no spunk'.

In fact the Triplanes did engage the Germans, but their formation broke up and 26-year-old Canadian Flt Sub-Lt Cuzner made the error of giving up his altitude advantage to square off with the more experienced von Richthofen. The latter subsequently reported, 'The aeroplane I had singled out caught fire and, after a short time, burned in the air and fell north of Henin Liétard'.

Cuzner was the baron's 52nd victory, and his only one over a Triplane. It was also the only victory credited to *Jasta* 11 during the course of a combat that nevertheless resulted in further British casualties. Separated from their flight, Arnold and Little spotted 'Naval 1's' patrol and a formation of five Albatros scouts below them. As both Triplanes dived, Little lost track of Arnold, only to see Minifie attacking an Albatros east of Douai. Little joined in and the German crash-landed on his aerodrome. The Australian then saw other Albatrosen attack Minifie, and 'although he put up a splendid fight, was forced down by numbers to about 50 ft, where I last saw him. I was then attacked by more scouts'.

Little fought his way out of this melee right above *Jasta* 11's base to share his tenth victory with Minifie, who also returned. Interviewed later in life, Minifie explained;

On 29 April 1917 19-year-old Victorian Flt Sub-Lt Richard P Minifie was credited with his first victory and a second shared with fellow Australian Bob Little. These successes came deep in the heart of the 'Red Baron's' domain, and Minifie claimed that his Triplane's superior speed helped him escape *Jasta* 11's wrath. He scored a total of 17 successes in Triplanes and four in Camels with 'Naval 1' prior to being brought down and captured on 17 March 1918 (*Mike Westrop*)

'Yes, they nearly had me down on Douai aerodrome – I was just 200-300 ft off it. Luckily, my Triplane was just a shade faster than they were. I was going low for home, and they let me go and get a lead of about 500 yards on them.'

More 'Naval 1' aces scored that evening. Flt Sub-Lt Forster Herbert Martin Maynard, a New Zealander from Waiuku who had joined the RNAS in 1915 and was just two days short of his 24th birthday, downed a D III OOC over Fresnoy. Rowley claimed a red Albatros OOC before three others shot up his engine, forcing him to glide over the lines and crash land south of Bapaume. Flt Sub-Lt H M D Wallace was less fortunate, being wounded in the arm and forced down south of Bapaume. He hastily burned his Triplane to prevent it falling into German hands, only to learn a short while later that he had, in fact, come down in Allied territory! Flt Sub-Lt Heywood was wounded, but he also made it home.

Although von Richthofen's men had managed to drive off the cheeky 'Tommies' who had violated their airspace, the Triplanes' overall performance left many of them stunned and the *Inspektion der Flieger* (*Idflieg*) concerned after reading reports about the new fighters. The RNAS, on the other hand, was pleased to let the exploits of its new heroes leak to the outside world.

'Bloody April's' last day was marked by a welter of RNAS activity, with 11 victories claimed. Two two-seaters fell to 'Naval 8's' Compston, as did two Albatros D IIIs to Little and one to Booker. Dallas of 'Naval 1' claimed a Rumpler and a D III. In Flanders, Collishaw of 'Naval 10' sent a D III crashing east of Cortemarck. In 'Naval 4', Australian Flt Sub-Lt C J Moir despatched an enemy aircraft OOC south of Nieuport and a new ace made his debut when Flt Sub-Lt Langley Frank Willard Smith sent an Albatros D II down OOC east of Nieuport.

Born in Philipsburg, Quebec, on 15 August 1897, Smith was living in Chicago when war broke out, and he was subsequently certified at the Curtiss Flying School at Newport News, Virginia, on 5 July 1916. From

Flt Lt Foster H M Maynard of 1 Naval Squadron sits in Triplane N5427, which bore the presentation *Philippine Britons No 1* on its port side. He used the aircraft to claim an Albatros D III OOC on 24 April 1917, this being the first of his six victories (*Fleet Air Arm Museum JMB/GSL06436*)

there he joined the RNAS in September and was assigned to 'Naval 4' in April 1917.

It had been a glorious month for 'Naval 3', with DSCs awarded to Breadner, Casey, Travers and Fall, and news arriving on 30 April that Jack Malone had been gazetted for the DSO. The day ended on a sour note, however, when Malone failed to return from his second sortie, escorting No 18 Sqn FE 2s and running into *Jasta* 12. Ironically, he was shot down by Ltn Paul Billik, a talented tyro who had only been with the *Staffel* a month. Malone was the first of his eventual 31 victories.

'It was thought that he had run into a large number of enemy aircraft when hunting away from his flight near Cambrai', Rochford recalled. 'Later, the Germans reported that he had been buried at Epinoy. During his quite short time with "Naval 3" Malone had shot down ten enemy aircraft, and I feel that had he lived, he would have become one of the great fighter pilots of the war. But he was essentially an individualist, and prone to leaving the formation to chase enemy aircraft on his own. This tendency eventually sealed his fate'.

A skilful and aggressive pilot with 'Naval 3', Canadian Flt Lt Joseph J Malone scored ten victories during the course of 'Bloody April' prior to being killed in action on the last day of that month. He was almost certainly the first victim of future German ace Ltn Paul Billik of *Jasta* 12 (*Norman Franks*)

—————— 'TRIPEHOUNDS' IN FULL STRIDE ——————

Impressed though the Germans may have been with the Sopwith Triplane's performance during 'Bloody April', the fierce combat that followed indicated that they were not intimidated, starting with two 'Naval 8' machines falling victim to Oblt Kurt von Döring of *Jasta* 4 and Wolff of *Jasta* 11 on 1 May. The best the squadron could do in return was a D III OOC by Little and a two-seater OOC by Compston on the 2nd.

'Naval 3's' Pups also saw action on 1 May whilst escorting No 18 Sqn FE 2s on a reconnaissance mission over Cambrai. 'There were lots of enemy aircraft about and "C" Flight was attacked soon after crossing the lines', Rochford recalled. 'I saw Armstrong sparring with a black Albatros Scout and I went to his aid. Together, we drove him down to 8000 ft, at which point we left him to pick up the FEs again'. The FE2s were miles ahead by now, and all three flights became too intensely embattled to catch up. 'However', Rochford noted, 'all's well that ends well and the FEs arrived home safely. Fall, with "B" Flight, shot down an enemy aircraft, but we lost Flt Sub-Lt A S Mather, who was reported missing in Pup N6186'.

The black Albatrosen 'Naval 3' encountered were from *Jasta* 12, which since von Osterroht's death had been commanded by Oblt Adolf *Ritter* von Tutschek. The latter had quickly introduced black tails and white spinners as a *Staffel* marking. Mather, who was captured, became von Tutschek's fifth victory, but Fall's claim over Epinoy may have been more than an 'OOC' for *Jasta* 12 recorded that Ltn Gerhard Strehl perished when his fighter was shot down in flames near that town.

The next day, Armstrong, Whealy and Pierce shared a two-seater in flames over Bourlon Wood and Casey, then leading 'A' Flight, claimed a D III OOC for his ninth victory. Awarded the DSC, Casey subsequently went on leave. Future ace Flt Sub-Lt Frederick Vincent Hall, who was born on 20 March 1898 in Muswell Hill, North London, and educated at Highgate School, teamed up with fellow 'Naval 4' pilot Flt Cdr J D Newberry to bring down a two-seater from FA 26. Its pilot, Ltn Karl Brill, was captured, but the wounded observer, Ltn d R Paul Reichel, died the next day.

Simpson of 'Naval 8' claimed a two-seater on 2 May, while on the 3rd squadronmate, and future ace, 19-year-old Flt Sub-Lt Phillip Andrew Johnston from Sydney, Australia, debuted with a D III OOC over Henin-Liétard.

'Naval 1' started May off with a D III destroyed on the 4th by Flt Cdr Cyril Askew Eyre. Born in England, and a graduate of Magdalen College, Oxford, Eyre was in Toronto when he joined the RNAS in 1915. He initially flew Pups in 'A' Naval Squadron prior to it becoming 1 Naval Squadron. Dallas and Culling each downed a D III the next day, and Minifie and Flt Sub-Lt Oliver B Ellis shared in an Albatros D II on the 11th.

Jasta 12 continued to be 'Naval 3's' nemesis, however. On 4 May von Tutschek brought Flt Sub-Lt H S Murton down in Rochford's Pup N6207, the RNAS pilot being captured. On the 11th Vfw Robert Riessinger downed Flt Sub-Lt J B Daniel, who also became a prisoner of war, while von Tutschek was credited with a second Pup, probably flown by Hubert Broad. 'He was "keeping an eye" on an enemy aircraft a few hundred yards away from him, and for some reason had his mouth wide open', Rochford wrote. 'The enemy pilot took a long range shot at him and a bullet entered Broad's mouth and passed straight out under his chin! He managed to land near Bapaume and was immediately rushed to hospital.'

In Flanders, '9 Naval' had been patrolling the coast with a complement of Pups that were just starting to be phased out by Triplanes. On 2 May 22-year-old Harold Francis Stackard from Muswell Hill teamed up with

In spite of this 'crack-up' caught on camera, Flt Sub-Lt Albert J Enstone did fairly well in 'Naval 4's' Pups, scoring four victories in N6187 between 9 May and 3 June and subsequently adding nine more to his tally in Camels (*Fleet Air Arm Museum JMB/GSL05836*)

19-year-old Harold Edgar Mott from Winnipeg, Manitoba, to destroy a two-seater near Middlekerke. Seven days later, Flt Lt Whealy, who had just been transferred to 'Naval 9' from 'Naval 3', downed a Halberstadt D II OOC. 'Naval 4's' Pups also scored on 9 May, including a balloon burned at Ghistelles by Smith, who then teamed up with Flt Lt Shook to destroy a two-seater that same evening, while another two-seater fell to 21-year-old Flt Sub-Lt Albert James Enstone from Birmingham.

'Naval 8' lost a Triplane on the 9th, but Little claimed a LVG and an Albatros that same day. The next day he downed another D III while Booker destroyed a two-seater and Compston and Flt Sub-Lt E A Bennetts shared another one between them. On the debit side Crundall was wounded by, but not credited to, Ltn Aloys Heldmann of *Jasta* 10. Simpson claimed two D Vs OOC the next day and Booker drove a D III down OOC on the 12th.

'Naval 4's' Pups scored on the 12th too, with Smith managing to destroy a D III off Zeebrugge. Enstone downed a Siemens-Schuckert (SSW) D I (a copy of the Nieuport 17), as did Flt Sub-Lt Geoffrey William Hemming from Worcester, who had joined the unit in April.

While the Pups struggled along, the Triplanes reasserted themselves. At 'Naval 10', Collishaw claimed a D III OOC east of Dixmude on 9 May and a floatplane off Ostend three days later. On the 15th, the squadron moved to Clairmarais for attachment to the RFC, while 'Naval 9' took its place at Furnes. Little of 'Naval 8' was credited with a DFW C V and an Albatros D III destroyed on the 18th.

'Naval 1' had mixed fortunes on 19 May. Culling downed a D III OOC, but Flt Sub-Lt Geoffrey G Bowman was killed when his fighter fell in flames after being targeted by von Tutschek of *Jasta* 12. During a scrap with *Jasta* 4 over Henin-Liétard that evening Eyre, Dallas, Gerrard and Minifie each added a D III OOC to their tallies, one of which might have resulted in Ltn Eberhard Fugner's death, but Ellis was killed by Ltn Gisbert-Wilhelm Groos.

Culling destroyed a two-seater on the 20th for his sixth victory – all of them claimed in Triplane N5444. 'Naval 3' Pups also scored as Rochford sent an Albatros down OOC and Nick Carter, by then commanding 'B' Flight, despatched a D III OOC for his fifth victory. On 23 May Flt Sub-Lt James Alpheus Glen, a 26-year-old Canadian from Ontario who had previously flown 1½ Strutters with 3 Naval Wing, scored his first with a D III OOC and Breadner claimed another.

'Naval 8's' Booker and Little jointly destroyed a D III on 23 May, while Simpson claimed another and Soar teamed up with Flt Sub-Lt Charles H B Jenner-Parsons to drive down a two-seater OOC. Flt Sub-Lt H A Pailthorpe was killed by Ltn Hans Hintsch of *Jasta* 11, however, while Flt Sub-Lt F V Hall, who had transferred in from 'Naval 4' on 5 May, was wounded – probably the unconfirmed Sopwith claimed by Offz Stv Paul Aue of *Jasta* 10 – and invalided out of the squadron.

'Naval 8' had a rematch with *Jasta* 11 over Douai the next morning, during which Booker claimed a D III in flames and shared two others with 23-year-old Flt Sub-Lt Roderick McDonald from St Joseph's, Nova Scotia. These coincided with *Jasta* 11's losses of Ltn Hintsch, who was killed, and Ltn Wilhelm Allmenröder, wounded, but Ltn d R Otto Masshoff shot down Flt Sub-Lt H L Smith.

Flt Sub-Lt James Alpheus Glen, holding a camera, and Frederick Carr Armstrong, facing the camera over his right shoulder, were both Canadians from Ontario who served long and well with 3 Naval Squadron in Pups and Camels (*Norman Franks*)

Triplane N6301 *DUSTY II* was used by Flt Lt Roderick McDonald of 'Naval 8' to down an Albatros D III OOC west of Douai on 28 May 1917. This was the third, and last, Triplane victory credited to the 24-year-old Nova Scotian, although he would score eight more times in Camels before being killed by Vfw Julius Trotsky of *Jasta* 43 on 8 May 1918. N6301, which later served with 10 and 1 Naval Squadrons, was destroyed by fire on 1 October 1917 (*Mike Westrop*)

Flt Lt Raymond Collishaw had claimed two victories in a Sopwith 1½ Strutter and two in a Pup by the time he took command of 'Naval 10's' 'B' Flight in April 1917. Influenced by the markings policy of 'C' Flight of 'Naval 3', he formed his own 'Black Flight', with an eye toward frontline notoriety – and Collishaw largely achieved his goal! Shuttleworth-built Triplane N533 '*BLACK MARIA*' (the first of six fitted with twin Vickers guns) was used by Collishaw to score the last two of his 34 Triplane victories on 27 July 1917 (*Norman Franks*)

On 25 May Little scored his 20th victory in the form of a D III. Chadwick of 'Naval 4' claimed a two-seater destroyed off Bray Dunes that morning, and several hours later he teamed up with Sub-Lts G H T Rouse, E W Busby and Langley Smith to down a Gotha 15 miles north of Westende, killing Oblt Manfred Messerschmidt *gennant* von Arnim and Ltn d Rs Willy Neumann and Werner Scholz of *Kampfstaffel* 13, *Kagohl* 3. Another future 'Naval 4' ace, 21-year-old Flt Sub-Lt Sydney Emerson Ellis from Kingston, Ontario, destroyed a D III southeast of Ghistelles for his first victory. Chadwick and Enstone downed a two-seater the next day.

On the 26th an LVG fell OOC to Flt Sub-Lt Oliver Colin Le Boutillier of 'Naval 9', who was at the controls of Triplane N5459. Born on 24 May 1894 in Montclair, New Jersey, 'Boots' Le Boutillier had been a student at Columbia University prior to deciding to enlist in the RNAS in July 1916.

The last day of May saw another future Canadian ace make his combat debut. Born in Regina, Saskatchewan, on 27 October 1893, Fred Everest Banbury was a law student who had flight qualified at Curtiss' school in the United States with the highest grades. Among the first contingent of 200 Canadians shipped to England for the RNAS, he joined 9 Naval Squadron in March 1917. On 31 May Banbury teamed

up with Flt Sub-Lts Stackard and A Shearer to drive a two-seater down OOC, and he started off the new month with a Halberstadt two-seater downed between Westende and Ghistelles.

───── 'NAVAL 10's' MONTH OF GLORY ─────

While other RNAS units saw varying degrees of action, the last Triplane-equipped unit, 10 Naval Squadron, was transitioning from being a pilot pool to a serious fighter outfit. On 21 April Sqn Cdr Bertram Bell ('Naval 3's' 'A' Flight leader with four victories) was appointed to command 'Naval 10'. His blunt abrasiveness afforded him scant popularity with his new pilots, but his administrative abilities, combined with an aggressive approach to combat, prepared the squadron for its commitment to support the British offensive in Flanders, to commence with the capture of the Messines-Wyschaete Ridge. Also contributing to the unit's readiness were suggestions by 'B' Flight commander Ray Collishaw regarding pilots to be posted out and promising talent to replace them.

No fewer than 13 of 'Naval 10's' 15 pilots at that time were Canadian, including all of Collishaw's hand-picked flight. His deputy, John Edward Sharman, had been born on 11 September 1892 in Oak Lake, Manitoba, and after joining the RNAS on 3 February 1916, he had flown 1½ Strutters in 3 Naval Wing, scoring his first victory on 25 February 1917. William Melville Alexander, born in Toronto on 8 November 1897, had also served in 3 Naval Wing, as had 22-year-old John Albert Page from Elizabethtown, Ontario, and Ellis Vair Reid, who, born in Belleville, Ontario, on 31 October 1889, was the oldest of the 'Black Flight' quintet.

One roster change occurred when Bell appointed 30-year-old Toronto native Flt Sub-Lt Arthur C Dissette to command 'C' Flight. Dissette, however, did not feel up to the task, and Bell insisted that Page support him as deputy. Collishaw reluctantly traded Page for Flt Sub-Lt Gerald Ewart Nash, born in Stoney Creek on 12 May 1896 and another 3 Naval Wing veteran.

On 15 May 'Naval 10' departed Furnes for Droglandt, where it fell under the command of No 11 Wing, 2nd Brigade, RFC. During subsequent patrols Nash, over whom Collishaw had initially favoured Page, engaged five Albatros D IIIs on the 21st and sent one down OOC between Ypres and Staden.

Meanwhile, the British Second Army prepared for its assault on Messines and the German *Luftstreiskräfte* moved more units into the sector, doubling its presence there by July. All ceased to be quiet over the Flanders Front as of 1 June, when Dissette and Page encountered an Aviatik and drove it down OOC. Reid claimed a two-seater in flames and Collishaw a scout. The latter, along with Alexander, Reid and Nash, sent a two-seater spinning down OOC the next morning, but Dissette failed to return, having probably fallen victim to Ltn Gustav Nolte of *Jasta* 18.

Collishaw claimed a D III in flames and Reid sent another crash-landing in a field on 3 June, but 'A' Flight lost its leader when Flt Sub-Lt Percy G McNeil was killed by Offz Stv Klein of *Jasta* 27. With the demoralising loss of two flight commanders in as many days, Bell reorganised his squadron into two flights for a few weeks, placing

Born in Belleville, Ontario, on 31 October 1889, Flt Sub-Lt Ellis Vair Reid joined the RNAS in 1915, flew Sopwith 1½ Strutters with 3 Naval Wing and became the second-ranking ace of Collishaw's 'Black Flight', with 19 successes between 1 June and 28 July 1917. He was killed by anti-aircraft fire on the latter date, however (*Norman Franks*)

Most popularly associated with Triplane N5487 *BLACK PRINCE*, in which he scored his first eight victories, William Melville Alexander was second to Collishaw in terms of total successes – 23 with 'Naval 10' and No 210 Sqn RAF in 465 combat hours – and the longest-lived of the 'Black Flight' pilots, dying in Toronto on 4 October 1988 (*Norman Franks*)

Sharman in charge of 'C' Flight and replacing him in 'B' Flight's ranks with 26-year-old Flt Sub-Lt Desmond Fitzgerald Fitzgibbon from Hampstead, London. The ambitious Sharman and Collishaw had not gotten along well, and although he occasionally alternated with Page, Sharman seems to have preferred leading 'C' to his old 'B' Flight.

While driving off an enemy reconnaissance aeroplane on 4 June, Fitzgibbon was shot up by an Albatros, but Alexander claimed another OOC. 'Naval 1' had also moved into the sector, where, during a dogfight with 15-20 enemy fighters on the 4th, Gerrard drove a D III down OOC and helped Capt Philip F Fullard of No 1 Sqn RFC send a second one to its destruction in flames. Their victim may have been Offz Stv Matthias Dennecke of *Jasta* 18, who was mortally wounded. Sydney Ellis of 'Naval' 4 also destroyed a D III.

Aerial activity in the Somme sector was by now on the wane, but Compston of 'Naval 8' still managed to down a two-seater OOC on 3 June. The following day he shared in the destruction of a two-seater (which was despatched in flames) with Flt Sub-Lts E A Bennetts and Ronald Roscoe Thornely. The latter, a veteran of Gallipoli with the Royal Naval Armoured Car Squadron, had joined the RNAS in May 1916 and been posted to 'Naval 8' the following March.

While sitting in his Pup on standby alert at an advanced landing ground the next day, Len Rochford of 'Naval 3' saw Nick Carter tangle with a balloon sited at its eastern end. Carter lived to describe the incident himself;

'My Pup in "Naval 3" had the words *Excuse Me* emblazoned on the fuselage, and it was quite the big joke when I ran into the balloon cable. That was a memorable episode. The kite balloon was at the ceiling of its cable height – about 7000 ft. I ran into the cable at a few hundred feet. The cable at this point and my engine got tangled, with the free end of the cable still attached to the balloon. The weight of my Pup was greater than the weight of the cable that was cut off, and the aircraft lowered the balloon a few hundred feet. The Pup landed a total wreck in a field downwind, N6474 being written off – the date was 4 June 1917.'

On 5 June Collishaw shared a two-seater in flames with Nash, Reid, Fitzgibbon and Flt Sub-Lt Kenneth G Boyd, and another OOC in concert with Fitzgibbon. Meanwhile, 'Naval 9's' Edgar Mott, still flying his old Pup N6193, destroyed a two-seater in flames off Ostend. At 1815 hrs that evening five Triplanes and two Pups of 'Naval 9' apparently encountered *Marine Feld Jagdstaffel* (MFJ) I off Ostend when the latter tried to rendezvous with 22 Gotha bombers returning from a raid on Sheerness, in Kent. The result was dubious claiming on both sides – a Triplane credited to Ltn zur See Theodor Osterkamp and an Albatros OOC each to Flt Sub-Lts Le Boutillier, John C Tanner and 19-year-old John William Pinder from Deal, in Kent.

'B' and 'C' Flights of 'Naval 10' engaged 20 enemy fighters over Polygon Wood on the 6th and Collishaw duly claimed two Albatros in flames and one OOC. Alexander drove another into a spinning nosedive, Nash sent a two-seater crashing and an Albatros OOC, and single scout claims went to Reid, Page, Sharman and Flt Sub-Lt John H Keens. That afternoon Hemming of 'Naval 4' destroyed an SSW D I and drove another down OOC northeast of Dixmude.

The Battle of Messines literally began with a bang at 0310 hrs on 7 June when 19 of the 21 mines the British had planted under the ridge went off, killing some 10,000 defenders. A short while later the Second Army, under Gen Herbert Plumer, advanced. The meticulous preparations made by Plumer's men were rewarded as the first objective was secured in three hours.

In the air that morning scouts were claimed by Collishaw and Nash, the latter achieving his fourth victory in just three days and his sixth overall. Reid sent a two-seater crashing near Clercken and Sharman claimed one scout destroyed and a second OOC before his Triplane, N6307, was damaged by gunfire, forcing him to land at Coudekerke. Roderick McDonald, on temporary loan from 'Naval 8', led a revived 'A' Flight, which included 'Teddy' Gerrard. The latter claimed a D III destroyed that morning for his ninth victory. Subsequently withdrawn for a rest, he was awarded the DSC and French CdG, and would score his tenth victory flying Camels with No 208 Sqn RAF on 6 April 1918. Having survived the war, Gerrard died in July 1923 after suffering a head injury when he fell from his horse during a polo match.

On 8 June 'Naval 1' lost Flt Lt Culling, killed by Vzflgmstr Bottler of MFJ I, and Flt Sub-Lt T R Swinburne, killed by Offz Stv Max Müller of *Jasta* 28. That afternoon Stackard of 'Naval 9' was credited with an Albatros OOC near Dixmude for his only Triplane victory, shortly after which he fell out of control himself and barely managed to recover at 400 ft before spinning into the ground, surviving with minor injuries.

'Naval 1' got into a scrap over Lens on 11 June, with Compston claiming a D III OOC that may have wounded Vfw Otto Rosenfeld of *Jasta* 12. That same day, over the Somme, Booker of 'Naval 8' claimed a D III, and on the 12th he, Jenner-Parsons and Soar brought down a two-seater near Arras. Ltn d R Franz Nieberle and Ltn Johannes von Pieverling of FA (A) 288b were captured.

An Albatros D V OOC on 13 June made an ace of 'Naval 1's' Rex Arnold. Awarded the DSC, he served as an instructor before returning to the front as a major in command of No 79 Sqn RAF, flying Sopwith Dolphins. Subsequently receiving the DFC as well as the Belgian CdG, Arnold remained in the RAF postwar, rising to the rank of group captain in January 1936.

'Naval 10' returned to action on the 14th, Sharman and Page each claiming a D III over Zonnebeke, but Flt Sub-Lt Leslie H Parker was killed by Vfw Fritz Krebs of *Jasta* 6. On 15 June Collishaw claimed a pair of two-seaters – one of which he shared with Sharman – and two Albatros D Vs, while Reid was credited with two D IIIs, Page claimed one and Fitzgibbon accounted for a Halberstadt and an Albatros. Booker of 'Naval 8' also downed a D V that day, while Eyre of 'Naval 1' brought a DFW C V of FA 7 down in Allied lines.

Compston of 'Naval 1' downed a two-seater on the 16th, while Little of 'Naval 8' teamed up with Johnston to destroy another, and Thornely and Compston brought one from FA (A) 211 down in Allied lines. Its pilot, Vfw Hermann Totsch, was killed in the crash but observer Ltn d R Friedrich Karl Riegel survived to be taken prisoner. Coming to the aid of some embattled No 23 Sqn SPADs on the 17th, Collishaw and Reid each downed an Albatros.

After scoring five victories in Pups with 'Naval 3', Canadian Flt Lt Alfred W Carter survived an extraordinary encounter with a kite balloon cable on 4 June 1917. Transferred to lead 'A' Flight of 'Naval 10' in July, he scored four victories in N6302 during the course of that month despite professing his dislike of Triplanes (*Norman Franks*)

Canadians John E Sharman and John A Page were destined to have similar careers with 'Naval 10'. Both scored seven victories within two months, both took on flight leaders' responsibilities and both were killed in action on the same day, 22 July 1917 (*Norman Franks*)

'Naval 10' squadronmates Flt Sub-Lts Raymond L Kent and Gerald E Nash were reunited in a PoW camp after Nash, a six-victory ace with Collishaw's flight, was brought down wounded in Triplane N5376 *BLACK SHEEP* on 25 June 1917 by Ltn Karl Allmenröder of *Jasta* 11, and Kent fell victim to Ltn Walter Blume of *Jasta* 26 on 11 July (*Mike Westrop*)

Poor weather and engine failures frustrated 'Naval 10' over the next few days, but 21 June saw Little of 'Naval 8' and Eyre of 'Naval 1' each down a D V. Two days later Sharman was promoted to flight lieutenant, while on the other side of the lines, Rittm Manfred von Richthofen took command of newly formed *Jagdgeschwader* I, which combined *Jastas* 4, 6, 10 and 11 into a permanent, mobile fighter wing to counter the aggressive British patrols.

On 24 June 'Naval 10's' pilots had their first encounter with what the Allies came to call the 'Flying Circus'. While escorting two DH 4s of No 57 Sqn on a photo-reconnaissance mission, which came under attack by 12 to 15 brightly painted scouts, Collishaw and Sharman each claimed a D V. Von Richthofen reported leading six *Jasta* 11 machines on that occasion, and he personally despatched DH 4 A3353, killing Capt Norman G McNaughton and Lt Angus H Mearns. Moreover, 'Naval 10's' Flt Sub-Lt Alan B Holcroft was captured after being wounded and Flt Sub-Lt Robert G Saunders killed, both men falling victim to Ltns Karl Allmenröder and Gisbert-Wilhelm Groos.

'Naval 10' suffered another loss on the 25th when Nash, in Triplane N5376 *Black Sheep*, became separated from his formation and was then attacked by Allmenröder. Wounded, he crash-landed behind German lines east of Messines and was captured. Gerald Nash went on to serve in the RCAF in World War 2, retiring as a group captain in 1945 and dying on 10 April 1976.

'Naval 8' finished off June with Little destroying a two-seater in flames east of Acheville on the 26th, killing Gefr Ernst Bittorf and Ltn d R Paul Schweizer of FA (A) 269, and Little and Soar downing a D V on the 29th.

ENTER THE CAMEL

Although the Germans were as dazzled by the performance of the Sopwith Triplane as its own pilots were delighted – enough for *Idflieg* to order every German manufacturer to come up with a triplane of its own – the agile fighter suffered from the same Achilles heel as its predecessor, the Pup. It was armed with only a single machine gun. This had not gone unnoticed by the Allies, and April 1917 had seen the combat debut of the SE 5a, with its Vickers and overwing Lewis guns, in the RFC, while the first SPAD XIII with twin Vickers also arrived for evaluation. In late

May 4 Naval Squadron received Britain's first scout with twin guns, the Sopwith F 1 Camel.

On 22 December 1916, T O M Sopwith, together with R J Ashfield, Herbert Smith, F Sigrist, and Harry Hawker, had unveiled the prototype F 1, which featured a shorter, deeper fuselage than the Pup. Its 130 hp Clerget rotary engine, cockpit and twin Vickers guns were all concentrated within the foremost seven feet of the fuselage. To facilitate production, Sopwith eliminated the dihedral on the upper wing while doubling the dihedral of the lower one to five degrees.

First tested on 26 December, the F 1 displayed dramatically different flight characteristics from those of the Pup and Triplane. The torque of its rotary engine, combined with the concentration of weight up front, endowed it with breathtaking manoeuvrability, but its sensitive controls required a judicious hand, especially during take-off.

When the third F 1 prototype was delivered to Martlesham Heath on 24 March 1917, RFC technical officer Sir Harry Tizard overheard one of the Testing Squadron's pilots say, 'Just to look at the beast gives me the hump at the thought of flying it'. That remark, along with the appearance of the aircraft's partially faired-over guns, led to the sobriquet 'Camel', which, although no more official than 'Pup', became just as universally used.

'Naval 4' wasted little time getting down to business with its new aeroplanes. On 4 June Flt Cdr Shook, in Camel N6347, attacked an enemy aircraft 15 miles off Nieuport, although it escaped in a sea haze. Engaging 15 German aircraft between Nieuport and Ostend the next evening, Shook sent a scout crashing onto the beach and drove a two-seater down OOC. The unit's first Camel loss occurred on 13 June when Langley Smith, who by then had eight victories in Pups to his name, was killed in N6362. Some witnesses said his Camel broke up while he was stunting above the German naval aerodrome at Neumünster.

FOCUS ON FLANDERS

Territorial gains during the Battle of Messines encouraged Gen Douglas Haig to prepare a follow-up offensive in Flanders, which was scheduled to commence on 25 July. Prior to the Fifth Army's advance, Nos 23, 29 and 32 Sqns RFC and 10 Naval Squadron were to launch an air offensive to deny the Germans as much aerial intelligence as possible. A sustained period of bad weather from 1 July seriously inhibited such activity, and the fighter squadrons were instead called upon to carry out low-level strafing attacks on enemy ground forces.

Flt Lt Collishaw got things going again on 2 July by destroying a two-seater. That same day Flt Lt Carter transferred in from 'Naval 3' to take charge of 'A' Flight.

On the 3rd 'Naval 1's' Flt Sub-Lt Cecil Guelph Brock, born in Southsea, Hampshire, on 24 May 1897 but residing in Winnepeg, Manitoba, when war broke out, drove a D III down OOC near Tenbrielen. That same day 'Naval 8's' Bob Little destroyed two D Vs, while Soar and Jenner-Parsons got one apiece.

'Naval 4's' Camels were also active, Chadwick sending a two-seater down OOC on 3 July. A prelude of different things to come occurred on the early morning of the 4th when five of 'Naval 4's' Camels encountered 16 Gothas 30 miles northwest of Ostend as they returned from a raid on England. Shook attacked one and last saw it diving and trailing black smoke. He then targeted a second bomber until his guns jammed. Shook was subsequently awarded the DSO for his actions. Dashing into the formation, Ellis fired 300 rounds at a Gotha, which then stalled and fell away trailing brown smoke from the rear gunner's cockpit. Enstone claimed to have damaged a Gotha and forced a second example down over the Netherlands.

'Naval 10's' 'B' Flight returned to form on 6 July when it found a formation of FE 2ds from No 20 Sqn beset by Albatros D Vs over Menin. Wading in, Collishaw claimed no fewer than six enemy aircraft OOC, which Sqn Cdr Bell recorded as one OOC and five 'apparently OOC'! Alexander was credited with three OOCs and Reid got another. For all the claims made by both the Triplane pilots and No 20 Sqn's gunners (they received credit for seven victories), the Germans only suffered one casualty, but it was a major one. Rittm Manfred von Richthofen was driven down with a head wound that would put him out of the war until the 25th. Ltn d R Alfred Niederhoff and Otto Brauneck of *Jasta* 11 followed the Baron down and landed near Wervicq, which may account for at least two of the OOC claims.

9 Naval Squadron, which had transferred to Flez aerodrome to relieve 'Naval 3' on 15 June, scored its only victory in the Somme sector on 7 July when Whealy, in Pup N6174, shared in driving a D V down

OOC with Pinder, Tanner, Mott and Flt Cdr H E Hervey. Tanner, however, was injured when his Pup was sent crashing in Allied lines by Ltn Fritz Anders of *Jasta* 4. Three days later 'Naval 9' returned to Bray Dunes and began re-equipping with Camels.

'Naval 3' had been replacing its Pups with Camels, too. 'On the morning of 7 July German raiders were again reported to be on their way to England, and at 1000 hrs we took off in an attempt to intercept them', 'Titch' Rochford recalled. 'We climbed northeastwards out to sea to a height of 18,000 ft. Twenty-five miles off Ostend we saw below us, at 10,000 ft, six enemy seaplanes. We dived on them and Joe Fall attacked one, firing into him at close range. Then Armstrong and I followed this seaplane as it dived down steeply, emitting clouds of smoke, to crash in the sea near a German destroyer, which opened fire on us. Fall attacked another seaplane, firing about 150 rounds at close range until it heeled over, slide-slipped and dived into the sea about a mile northwest of Ostend Pier, leaving a trail of blue smoke in the sky. A third seaplane was attacked by Glen from underneath, firing 150 rounds at close range. This one dived straight into the sea and sank almost immediately, only pieces of the aeroplanes remaining on the surface of the water.'

Flying Pup N6479, Fall shared his first floatplane with Rochford, Glen, Armstrong and Flt Sub-Lt R F P Abbott, as well as Flt Sub-Lt Ellis of 'Naval 4'. He shared the second with Glen. An hour later Fall shot a D V down in flames for his 11th victory – a record for the Pup.

The Gotha raid that had drawn 'Naval 3' seaward had also attracted the wrath of Sopwith Triplanes on Home Defence duty, including N5382 flown by 19-year-old Flt Sub-Lt Rowan Heywood Daly from Leigh-on-Sea, Essex. Taking off from Manston and giving chase to a Gotha G III, he shot it down in flames 15 miles off Ostend and was subsequently awarded the DSC for his actions. Its crewmen, Ltn Hans Richter, Ltn d R Max Röselmüller and Vfw Wilhelm Weber of *Kampfstaffel* 13/ *Kagohl* 3, were killed.

7 July also saw one ace's career with 'Naval 1' end and another's begin. Flt Cdr Eyre was credited with an Albatros OOC and one in flames, bringing his total to six, before he was killed – possibly a double claim credited to both Ltn Niederhoff of *Jasta* 11 and Vfw Friedrich Altemeir of *Jasta* 24. Flt Sub-Lts H K Millward and D W Ramsey were also shot down by Ltn Wolff of *Jasta* 11 and Ltn Richard Krüger of *Jasta* 4. Finally,

As previously mentioned in this volume, Triplane N5493 had been Flt Lt Bob Little's *BLYMP* in 'Naval 8' during the spring and early summer of 1917. It is seen here in August 1917 after being repaired following damage inflicted in combat on 28 July. No longer assigned to Little, the aircraft has had its nickname removed from beneath the cockpit, a white border applied to its fuselage cockade and a red heart added to its fin. Little scored his last Triplane victory (an Albatros D V OOC) in N5493 on 10 July. Parked alongside the fighter is N6290 *DIXIE LEE*, which Flt Lt Rex A Arnold had used to send an Albatros D III OOC on 3 May, followed by a D V OOC on 13 June for his fifth, and final, success (*Fleet Air Arm Museum JMB/GSL06469*)

a D V was credited OOC to Flt Sub-Lt Anthony George Allen Spence, a 20-year-old graduate of Toronto University. This was the first of his eventual nine victories.

Bob Little downed a D V on 10 July for his 28th victory overall and his 24th, and last, in a Triplane, as Camels had been arriving at 'Naval 8' since late June. 'Naval 4's' Camels were also in action on the 10th, engaging four D Vs over Pervyse. Chadwick was credited with one OOC, and he shared in the destruction of another with 22-year-old Flt Sub-Lt Ronald McNeill Keirstead from Wolfeville, Nova Scotia. Flt Sub-Lt Busby was killed over Ramscapelle by Vfw Georg Strasser of *Jasta* 17, however, his Camel (N6361) being the first to fall victim to a German fighter.

Soar of 'Naval 8' was flying a Camel on 11 July when he and Flt Sub-Lt J H Thompson brought down a two-seater of FA (A) 235 east of Izel-le-Hameau. Its pilot, Uffz Max Marczinke, was badly wounded and the rear gunner, Uffz Kurt Prüfer, succumbed to his wounds. Collishaw and Alexander of 'Naval 10' added an Albatros each to their scores that evening, but Flt Sub-Lt Raymond L Kent was brought down by Ltn Walter Blume of *Jasta* 26 and captured.

During a running fight with the enemy on 12 July, Reid claimed two antagonists and Collishaw one, but Flt Sub-Lt Charles R Pegler was killed by Ltn Wolfgang Güttler of *Jasta* 24. Shortly after noon Sharman downed a scout for his eighth victory. Several hours earlier Minifie of 'Naval 1' had become an ace with two D Vs OOC. Little of 'Naval 8', now in Camel N6378, also enjoyed success on the 12th when he drove a D V down OOC. 'Naval 4', however, was reminded of what a double-edged sword the Camel's flying characteristics could be when five-victory ace Sidney Ellis took off, suddenly fell into a spin and fatally crashed.

On 13 July Little and Soar despatched a two-seater and the former also caught a D V diving on a SPAD over Oppy. Firing 200 rounds at it, he sent the Albatros down OOC, after which he got a wave of thanks from the SPAD pilot – fellow Aussie and future six-victory ace Lt Claud R J Thompson of No 19 Sqn. Two other Germans fell OOC to Phillip Johnson. One, a Rumpler, was shared with Flt Sub-Lt William Lancelot Jordan, a 21-year-old Londoner who had worked his way up from air mechanic to observer to pilot during his time in the RNAS.

'Naval 8's' Soar had reverted to Triplane N6292 when he and Booker downed an Albatros OOC on 17 July. Five 'Naval 9' pilots shared in a D V OOC over Nieuport that day, including Le Boutillier and Flt Lt Edmond Pierce, who had transferred in from 'Naval 3'. Finally, Carter downed a D V OOC for his first Triplane victory since being transferred to 'Naval 10'.

One more Canadian of some note scored his first victory on the 17th. Born in Carleton Place, Ontario, on 23 December 1893, Arthur Roy Brown had qualified as an RNAS pilot on 24 November 1915. Injured in a crash on 2 May 1916, he was assigned in quick succession to 9, 11, 4 and 11 Naval Squadrons following his recovery. The latter unit, formed in Dunkirk in March 1917, was essentially a training and holding squadron, but while Brown was flying Pup N6174 on 17 July he encountered an Albatros and drove it down OOC for his first victory. 'Naval 11' was dissolved in August, only to be re-formed in March 1918

On 10 July Nova Scotian Flt Sub-Lt Ronald McNeill Keirstead of 'Naval 4' shared in the destruction of an Albatros D V southeast of Nieuport with fellow Canadian Flt Lt Arnold J Chadwick for his first of an eventual 13 victories (*Norman Franks*)

Triplan "Sopwith"
Moteur rotatif.

Flt Lt C D Booker's Triplane N5482 is refuelled sometime after its fuselage cockade was given a white surround in accordance with a policy adopted in July 1917, which also resulted in a change to the fuselage band. The aeroplane retains the legend *MAUD* beneath the cockpit, along with a small personal marking that cannot be identified. This is almost certainly how Booker's Triplane looked when he wounded *Jasta* 12 leader Oblt Adolf *Ritter* von Tutschek on the evening of 11 August 1917 (*Colin Huston/Cross & Cockade International*)

with DH 9s and serve out the rest of the war as No 211 Sqn RAF. Brown, meanwhile, was finally assigned to 'Naval 9', where he would find his niche in World War 1 lore.

After two days of prohibitive weather, 'Naval 10' resumed scoring on the 20th, with Collishaw and Reid driving D Vs down OOC, Alexander claiming one in flames and Little teaming up with three 'Naval 8' mates to despatch a DFW C V also in flames. The following day Collishaw claimed two D Vs OOC and Reid one destroyed, while Little downed a D V OOC over Oppy.

'Naval 6', which had moved to Bray Dunes and replaced its Nieuports with Camels in late June, had undertaken numerous patrols when Flt Lt Winter downed an Albatros on 21 July. The next day Flt Lt de Roeper sent a two-seater spinning down and a D V fell to Flt Sub-Lt Maxwell Hutcheon Findlay. Born in Aberdeen, Scotland, on 17 February 1899, Findlay was living in Canada when war drew him back to enlist in the Black Watch and later transfer to the RNAS.

After receiving the DSC and being put in command of 'Naval 1' on 14 June, Dallas destroyed an Albatros two-seater near Lille on 22 July. 'Naval 8's' Thornely downed a D III OOC and Johnston became an ace that morning by destroying a D III, probably killing Vfw Georg Oefele of *Jasta* 12. Later in the day Little of 'Naval 8' was credited with a two-seater and a D V OOC, while Soar scored his 12th, and final, victory (an Albatros) in concert with Booker. Subsequently awarded the DSC, Soar died in 1971.

The 22nd was an unhappy day for 'Naval 10', however. During a fight with *Jasta* 11, John Sharman's Triplane N6307 broke up – credited to Oblt Wilhelm Reinhard, but more likely struck by a shell from *Flak Batterie* 503 – and John Page, in N5478, was slain by Ltn Otto Brauneck. Reid and Carter extracted a small measure of revenge on the 23rd with D Vs OOC. Carter downed another on the 24th, but that evening Flt Sub-Lt Theodore C May was killed by Ltn Helmuth Dilthey

Flt Sub-Lt William H Chisam poses with a Pup while on Home Defence duty with 'Naval 3' at Walmer, in Kent. During a Fleet Protective Patrol on 26 July 1917, 'B' Flight was attacked over Ostend by four Albatros D Vs. Flt Sub-Lt J A Glen drove one down, but Chisam force-landed his Camel on the beach near Coxyde Bains with its engine and controls damaged. His was probably the Camel claimed by, but not confirmed to, Flgmstr Bertram Heinrich of *Marine Feld Jasta* I. Chisam went on to score seven victories between 3 September 1917 and 24 March 1918 (*Norman Franks*)

Born in Havelock North, New Zealand, on 7 July 1896, Harold Francis Beamish joined the RNAS in June 1916. Assigned to 3 Naval Squadron on 9 January 1917, 'Kiwi' Beamish scored his first victory in Pup N6202 on 23 April. His next success came in Camel N6377 on 27 July, when he and four squadronmates destroyed a German floatplane 20 miles off Ostend. Beamish, who was ultimately credited with a total of 11 victories, subsequently led 'A' Flight of No 203 Sqn RAF and received the DSC. He raised sheep and cattle at Whana Whana until his death on 26 October 1986 (*Norman Franks*)

of *Jasta* 27. Flt Cdr George Simpson, who had transferred to 'Naval 9' in June, drove a two-seater down OOC that day.

The British offensive had been scheduled for 25 July, as previously noted, but it was postponed until the 28th. Meanwhile, Chadwick, Enstone and Keirstead of 'Naval 4' shared in the destruction of one of nine floatplanes they encountered 30 miles north of Ostend. A two-seater was also driven down OOC off Westende by 'Naval 9' Camels flown by Flt Lt Banbury and Flt Sub-Lts Pinder, Mott, Snell and Oliver William Redgate, an 18-year-old arrival from Nottingham. Mott, for whom this was his fifth victory, left 'Naval 9' later in the year. He died in Brantford, Ontario, on 27 January 1992.

On 26 July Bell reorganised 10 Naval Squadron once again, placing Alexander in charge of 'C' Flight. The next day saw heavy activity, with Roderic McDonald, who had returned to 'Naval 8', and Little destroying a two-seater near Loos, killing Uffz Heinrich Jourgens and Ltn d R Alexander Köhler of FA (A) 240. This was McDonald's fifth victory and Little's last before going on a well-deserved rest leave. In August the Australian ace received a DSO and a Bar for his DSC, to which would be added a Bar to the DSO the following month.

'Naval 3', based at Furnes, replaced the last of its Pups in mid-July. During a fleet protective patrol on 27 July, 'B' Flight drove off four German two-seaters carrying torpedoes and shot their single-seat floatplane escort into the sea off Ostend. Credit was shared between

Glen, Fall, Beamish and two 20-year-olds destined for future acedom, Flt Sub-Lt Louis Drummond Bawlf from Winnipeg, Manitoba, and Marlborough-educated Flt Sub-Lt Aubrey Beauclerk Ellwood.

At 'Naval 6', Flt Sub-Lt James Henry Forman, born in Kirkfield, Ontario, on 1 February 1896, claimed a D V in flames northeast of Nieuport on the 27th, probably killing Vzflgmstr Otto Brandt of MFJ I. Forman was wounded in the shoulder the next day, and upon his recovery he was reassigned to 'Naval 1' on 29 September. 27 July also saw Collishaw, flying newly

acquired N533 (one of six Triplanes experimentally fitted with two machine guns), destroy one opponent and drive a second down OOC. Carter also claimed an OOC, but Flt Sub-Lt Gerald Roach was killed by Ltn Karl-August von Schönebeck of *Jasta* 11.

10 Naval Squadron's 'Black Flight' had by now made an indelible name for itself, but its moment of glory came to a sudden end on 28 July. Ray Collishaw, credited with 30 victories in two months, was posted to Canada on leave, Mel Alexander claimed a D V OOC over Dadizeele for his eighth, and last, victory in Triplane N5487 *Black Prince* and Ellis Reid, in N5483 *Black Roger*, destroyed a D V but did not return. He had been killed by *K Flak* 21 near Armentières. For the next few weeks 'B' Flight ceased to exist.

Jordan and Thornely of 'Naval 8' also enjoyed success on the 28th, each pilot downing an Albatros scout OOC, as did Winter of 'Naval 6', while a two-seater fell to Simpson in concert with 19-year-old Flt Sub-Lt Francis John William Mellersh. 'Naval 4' lost another ace that day when Arnold Chadwick, whose score had reached 11 on 26 July, had to ditch his Camel off La Panne and drowned before he could be rescued. His DSC was gazetted a month later.

The British Flanders offensive had been rescheduled for the 28th. However, bad weather, combined with French difficulties in bringing up their supporting artillery, postponed it further until 31 July.

On 29 July Whealy, who had transferred to 'Naval 9' in May, was flying Triplane N5490 when he sent a D V down OOC and despatched another in flames. Le Boutillier also downed a D III OOC that day, to which he would add six victories with No 209 Sqn

Camel B3782 of 'Naval 3' was used by Flt Sub-Lt J A Glen to down a floatplane on 27 July 1917 and by Flt Lt Lloyd S Breadner to complete his scoring with two Albatros D Vs destroyed on 3 September and another sent down OOC eight days later. Subsequently transferred to 'Naval 13', B3782 was being flown by Flt Lt John deC Paynter when he shared in the destruction of a floatplane on 29 January 1918, an Albatros two-seater the next day and another floatplane on 19 February. 'Naval 13' became No 213 Sqn RAF on 1 April 1918, and B3782 was finally written off in a crash while still with the unit on the 20th of that month (*Fleet Air Arm Museum JMB/GSL06394*)

'Naval 4's' Flt Lt Arnold Jacques Chadwick scored his first victory on 26 April 1917, and he downed a total of five enemy aeroplanes flying Pups and another six in Camels. On 28 July 1917 Chadwick drowned after he was forced to ditch Camel N6369 in the sea off La Panne (*Norman Franks*)

47

RAF in 1918, and subsequently pursue a long and varied postwar aviation career before dying in Las Vegas, Nevada, on 12 May 1983.

Also on the 29th three 'Naval 8' Triplanes, flown by Booker, Crundall and Flt Sub-Lt Stanley W McCrudden, were jumped by ten D Vs of *Jasta* 12. Crundall was evading in a climbing turn when he accidentally flicked his blip switch, stalling both engine and aeroplane. Falling into a spinning nosedive, Crundall waited until the Germans – convinced he was doomed – broke off their pursuit, then pulled up near the ground and crossed the trenches at low level. His bullet-riddled Triplane was credited as victory No 20 for von Tutschek, who within the month would run into 'Naval 8' one time too many.

— 'TRIPEHOUND'S' TOO-LONG LAST HURRAH —

August 1917 saw the Sopwith Camel replace the Pup and Triplane in RNAS frontline units, but not without a few notable parting shots from the latter. Minifie of 'Naval 1', for example, flew one to claim a D V in flames on the 8th. 'Naval 8' Camel pilots Jordan and Thornely shared credit for a D V the following day, while Brock and Spence of 'Naval 1'

Born in Ruabon, North Wales, on 23 January 1893, Flt Lt Howard J T Saint scored four victories in Triplanes and three in Camels with 'Naval 10'. His rapid rise to flight command in August 1917 reflected the attrition his unit was suffering, and his imprudent leadership qualities led to more than one squadron misfortune (*Mike Westrop*)

Flt Lt Francis D Casey assumes a cocky pose in front of a Camel upon returning to 'Naval 3' from leave. Consummate flier though he was, Casey was killed while 'stunting' a Camel on 11 August 1917. Len Rochford noticed 'Red' Mulock leave two wreaths by his grave at Coxyde, the ace noting that 'One was from himself and the other from Kathryn Martyn, a young actress who was then in one of the London shows and to whom, I believe, Casey was engaged' (*Norman Franks*)

also downed one apiece. Brock would bring his total to seven in 1918 with Nos 209 and 3 Sqns RAF. He eventually passed away in Toronto on 20 February 1967.

At noon on the 9th, a 'Naval 10' patrol was ambushed over Polygon Wood by four Albatros scouts. Flt Lt Howard John Thomas Saint, a 24-year-old from Ruabon, North Wales, who had served with the Royal Naval Armoured Cars in France prior to undertaking flight training in 1916, initially flew bombers with 'Naval 5' before joining 10 Naval Squadron on 26 July. He turned on one assailant and drove it down OOC, although squadronmate Flt Sub-Lt Keith R Munro fell victim to Ltn d R Güttler of *Jasta* 24.

Maynard of 'Naval 1' was credited with OOCs on the 9th and 10th, bringing his total to six. He was subsequently posted to the Air Depot at Dunkirk in September. Injured in a crash in England, he survived the war with the rank of captain, remained in the RAF through World War 2 and retired as an air vice-marshal.

'Naval 3' began 11 August with the tragic loss of its Irish ace, Francis Casey. 'He had been on leave in England and returned to Furnes on the evening of the previous day', Rochford recalled. 'Soon after breakfast he took off in his Camel and, as was usual with him, commenced doing "stunts" at a very low altitude. He did side-loops and spins, each time pulling out of the dive just above the ground. Eventually, he put his machine into a spin at a height too low from which to recover and he crashed in a field across the road which ran past the aerodrome. He was unconscious when put on a stretcher and into the ambulance, which took him to the hospital in La Panne. He was operated on at once for a fracture of the base of the skull, but he died in the afternoon and was buried in the cemetery at Coxyde that same evening'.

'Naval 8' had another run-in with *Jasta* 12 on the 11th. Booker, still flying his Triplane N5482 *Maud*, and Jordan in Camel N6372 shot down a D V whose pilot, none other than *Staffelführer* von Tutschek, was hospitalised with a shoulder wound. Booker was in turn set upon by two more Albatros scouts and forced to land his badly damaged aeroplane at Farbus, his demise being credited to Ltn d R Viktor Schobinger.

During a morning patrol by 'Naval 10' on 12 August, 23-year-old Flt Sub-Lt George Leonard Trapp from New Westminster, British Columbia, downed an Albatros OOC, as did Flt Sub-Lt Harold Day, a 20-year-old Welshman from Abergavenny. That evening, Harold Kerby, who had departed 'Naval 3' to fly Pups in Home Defence from Walmer aerodrome in Kent, attacked Gotha G IV 656/16, which had bombed Margate, and sent it crashing into the sea off Southend. He was awarded the DSC following this success. Uffz Rudolf Stolle, Ltn Hans Rolin and Uffz Otto Rosinsky of *Kampfstaffel* 16/*Kagohl* 3 were killed. Kerby repeated that performance ten days later during the last Gotha daylight raid on Britain, downing G IV 663/16 of *Kampfstaffel* 15/*Kagohl* 3 off Margate. Ltn d R Werner Joschkowitz and Ltn Walter Latowski drowned, but Uffz Bruno Schneider was rescued by the destroyer HMS *Kestrel*. Continuing his career in the RAF postwar and attaining the rank of group captain in 1939, Kerby died in London on 8 June 1963.

A new 'Naval 1' ace made his debut on 14 August when Stanley Wallace Rosevear downed a D V OOC northeast of Ypres, while Ridley

During a morning patrol by 'Naval 10' on 12 August 1917, Welsh-born Flt Sub-Lt Harold Day, in Triplane N5437, downed an Albatros D V OOC. He would score the rest of his 11 victories flying Camels with 'Naval 8' (*Norman Franks*)

After claiming seven victories in Pups with 'Naval 3', Flt Lt Harold S Kerby was commanding a Home Defence unit at Walmer when he destroyed a Gotha G IV off Southend on 12 August 1917. Ten days later, flying the same Pup (N6440), he downed a second Gotha off Margate, bringing his tally to nine. Attaining the RAF rank of group captain in 1939, Kerby died in London on 8 June 1963 (*N Franks*)

Bringing down his first opponent with 'Naval 1' on 14 August 1917, Flt Sub-Lt Stanley W Rosevear was still flying Triplane N5489 when he scored victories five through eight between 17 and 24 October. Re-opening his account in a Camel on 5 December, he ultimately brought his tally to 25 on 22 April 1918 (*Norman Franks*)

On 22 August 1917, just five days after joining 'Naval 4', Flt Sub-Lt Adrian J B Tonks drove two Albatros D Vs down OOC southeast of Ostend. Born in Kensington, London, on 10 May 1898, Tonks scored ten more victories and survived the war with a DFC and Bar, only to die of injuries following a flying accident on 14 July 1919 (*Norman Franks*)

accounted for another. Born in Walkerton, Ontario, on 9 March 1896, Rosevear had attended the University of Toronto prior to joining the RNAS in February 1917.

On the same day, Saint led three 'Naval 10' Triplanes down after three Albatrosen, only to be jumped by five more. In the course of fighting their way out of the trap, Saint despatched an assailant in flames, but Flt Sub-Lt Seisyllt H Lloyd, flying twin-gun Triplane N536, was killed by Uffz Karl Theodor Steudel of *Jasta* 3.

After leading a last patrol on the 15th, Nick Carter departed on rest leave to Canada. Sqn Cdr Bell shifted Alexander to his slot in command of 'A' Flight and gave 'C' Flight to Saint.

Fall of 'Naval 3' was credited with a D V OOC on the 17th, but 'Naval 8' lost an ace when Flt Cdr Phillip Johnston collided with Flt Sub-Lt Bennetts. Both men were killed, their demise being credited to the German attacking them at the time, Oblt Hans Bethge of *Jasta* 30. Keirstead of 'Naval 4' claimed a D V the following day, while Booker and Crundall of 'Naval 8' shared their last Triplane victory (yet another D V OOC) with Flt Lt Richard Burnard Munday, a future ace from Plymouth. Crundall subsequently raised his score to seven leading a flight in No 210 Sqn in 1918, receiving the DFC. He would write of his long career in both the RAF and civil aviation in a 1975 autobiography, *Fighter Pilot on the Western Front*.

Alexander of 'Naval 10' was flying a Camel when he downed a D V on 18 August, as were 'Naval 8's' Jordan, Thornely, McDonald and Thompson when they shared credit for a DFW destroyed on the 19th. On 20 August Findlay of 'Naval 6' downed a D V, while De Roeper drove down a two-seater for his fifth, and final, victory. The latter served as an instructor with various training units in France until war's end, after which he was gazetted for the Air Force Cross on 3 June 1919. Rising to the rank of group captain in the postwar RAF, De Roeper died on 1 August 1965.

Alexander was back in a Triplane – N6302, as flown by his predecessor, Carter – when he added two D Vs to his bag on 20 and 21 August. Trapp also claimed an Albatros and Saint a two-seater on the 21st, while 24-year-old Flt Sub-Lt John Gerald Manuel from Winnipeg, who had previously served in the Canadian Field Artillery, was credited with the destruction of a D V and another sent down OOC.

E T Hayne of 'Naval 3' scored his first victory, a DFW OOC, on 22 August. That same day two new 'Naval 4' aces, both 19, made their debuts. Flt Sub-Lt Adrian James Boswell Tonks from Kensington, London, had only joined the squadron five days earlier, but he drove two adversaries down OOC southeast of Ostend, and Charles Robert Reeves Hickey from Parksville, British Columbia, who had previously served with the Canadian Mounted Rifles, got another. Hemming also claimed three D Vs, bringing his tally to six and earning him both the DSC and CdG, but he would add no more victories prior to leaving the squadron in June 1918.

Saint and Fitzgibbon of 'Naval 10' each claimed a D V OOC during another run-in with the 'Flying Circus' on the 25th, but Flt Sub-Lt Alfred D M Lewis was brought down by Ltn Hans-Georg von der Osten of *Jasta* 11 and captured. August ended with 'Naval 10' reduced to just nine pilots and Saint, in spite of having occasionally led his flight into enemy traps, promoted to flight lieutenant.

1 September marked the combat debut of the Fokker F I (the only fighter created in response to *Idflieg's* call for a Sopwith Triplane copy to be built in significant numbers) when Manfred von Richthofen used it to shoot down an RE 8 whose crew probably mistook it for an RNAS scout. Aside from its three-wing configuration and rotary engine, the Fokker differed radically from its British counterpart, featuring a wooden box cantilever structure that obviated wire bracing.

Ironically, even as the Fokker triplane began its rise to somewhat overrated fame, the Sopwith Triplane had been withdrawn from most frontline units in favour of the two-winged, twin-gun Camel. An equally ironic exception was 'Naval 1', the first unit to get the Triplane and destined to keep it long past its prime.

That did not seem to dampen Richard Minifie's élan. He destroyed D Vs on 16 and 19 September and a two-seater on the 26th. On 17 October he despatched a DFW, drove a Gotha down OOC on the 18th, a D V OOC on the 20th, claimed a 'Fokker D V' destroyed on the 27th and a two-seater on the 31st. Minifie received the DSC on 2 November.

Samuel Kinkead also soldiered on in the Triplane to down DFWs on 17 September and 17 October, as well as one shared on the 18th with Flt Sub-Lt Forman, for whom, after his first victory in a Camel with 'Naval 6', the Triplane must have seemed a retrograde step. Kinkead downed a two-seater on 24 October and a D V five days later, both with the Triplane. Forman, however, had a Camel on 12 November when he and Kinkead jointly despatched a Pfalz D III in flames, probably killing Obflgmt Karl Meyer of MFJ I.

Among other pilots in 'Naval 1' to claim the Triplane's final successes were Ridley, with a DFW downed on 10 September, and Rosevear, who achieved victories over D Vs on 19 September and 17 and 21 October, as well as two two-seaters destroyed on 24 October. Spence claimed two-seaters OOC on 21 and 26 October and Rowley got one on 13 November.

These Triplane pilots of 'Naval 1' at Bailleul in July 1917 are, from left to right, S M Kinkead, J H Foreman, H Wallace, A G A Spence, H L Everitt, H V Rowley, Luard, McGrath, E D Crundall, W H Sneath, Burton, A R McAfee, S W Rosevear, R P Minifie, R S Dallas, C B Ridley, J S deWilde, White and E B Holden (*Norman Franks*)

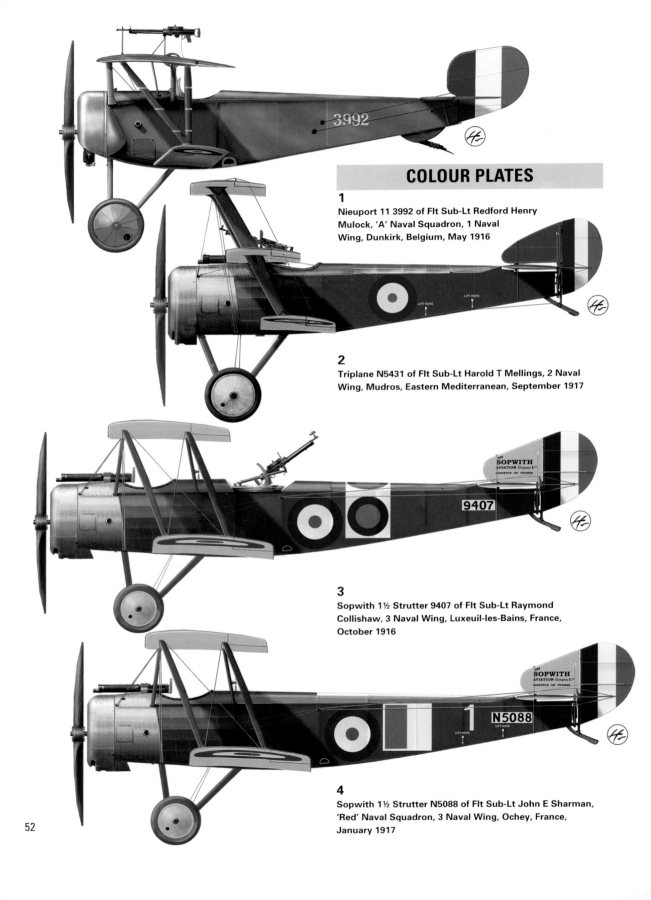

COLOUR PLATES

1

Nieuport 11 3992 of Flt Sub-Lt Redford Henry
Mulock, 'A' Naval Squadron, 1 Naval
Wing, Dunkirk, Belgium, May 1916

2

Triplane N5431 of Flt Sub-Lt Harold T Mellings, 2 Naval
Wing, Mudros, Eastern Mediterranean, September 1917

3

Sopwith 1½ Strutter 9407 of Flt Sub-Lt Raymond
Collishaw, 3 Naval Wing, Luxeuil-les-Bains, France,
October 1916

4

Sopwith 1½ Strutter N5088 of Flt Sub-Lt John E Sharman,
'Red' Naval Squadron, 3 Naval Wing, Ochey, France,
January 1917

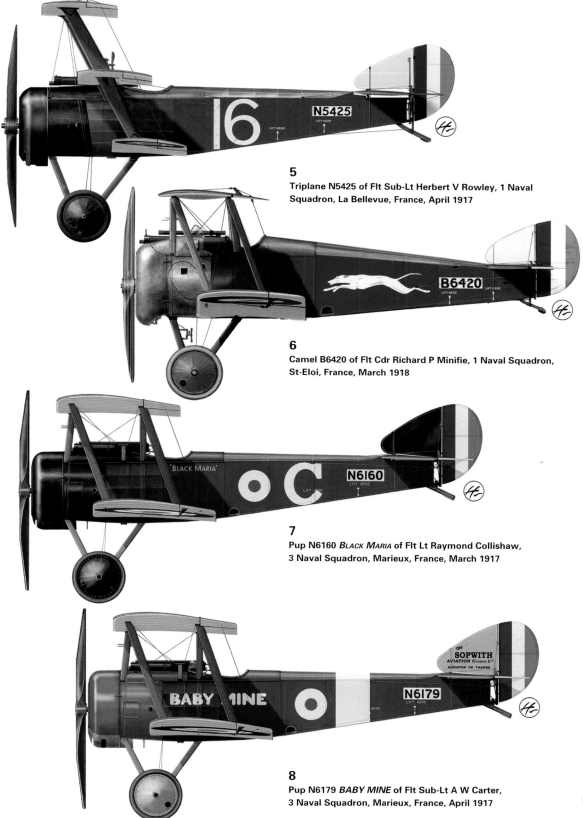

5
Triplane N5425 of Flt Sub-Lt Herbert V Rowley, 1 Naval
Squadron, La Bellevue, France, April 1917

6
Camel B6420 of Flt Cdr Richard P Minifie, 1 Naval Squadron,
St-Eloi, France, March 1918

7
Pup N6160 *BLACK MARIA* of Flt Lt Raymond Collishaw,
3 Naval Squadron, Marieux, France, March 1917

8
Pup N6179 *BABY MINE* of Flt Sub-Lt A W Carter,
3 Naval Squadron, Marieux, France, April 1917

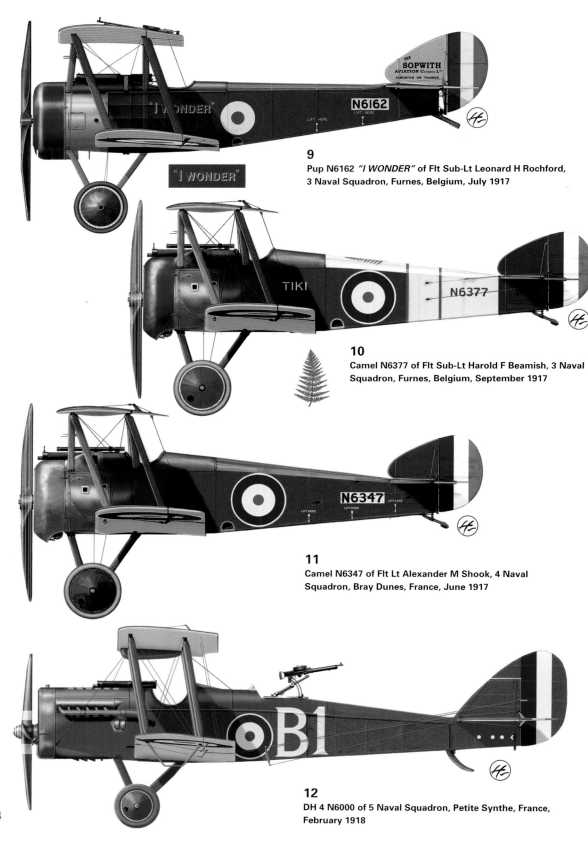

9
Pup N6162 *"I WONDER"* of Flt Sub-Lt Leonard H Rochford,
3 Naval Squadron, Furnes, Belgium, July 1917

10
Camel N6377 of Flt Sub-Lt Harold F Beamish, 3 Naval
Squadron, Furnes, Belgium, September 1917

11
Camel N6347 of Flt Lt Alexander M Shook, 4 Naval
Squadron, Bray Dunes, France, June 1917

12
DH 4 N6000 of 5 Naval Squadron, Petite Synthe, France,
February 1918

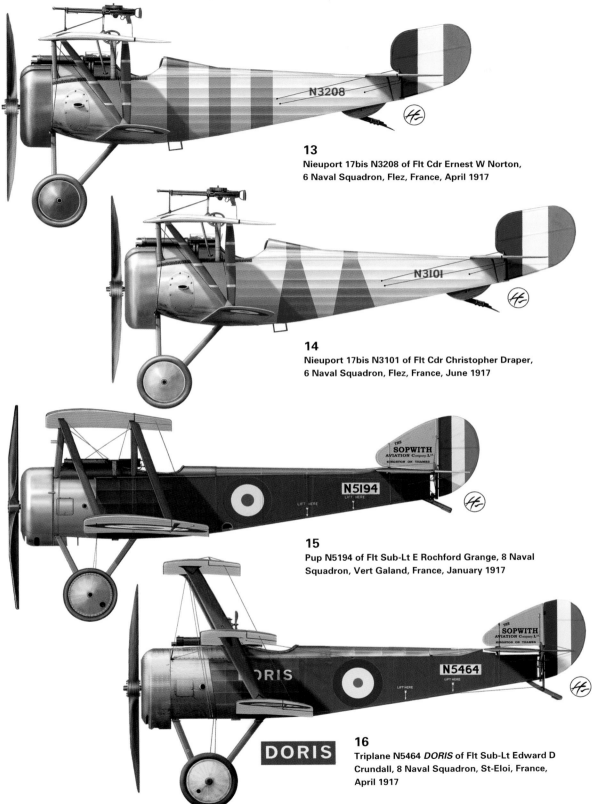

13
Nieuport 17bis N3208 of Flt Cdr Ernest W Norton,
6 Naval Squadron, Flez, France, April 1917

14
Nieuport 17bis N3101 of Flt Cdr Christopher Draper,
6 Naval Squadron, Flez, France, June 1917

15
Pup N5194 of Flt Sub-Lt E Rochford Grange, 8 Naval
Squadron, Vert Galand, France, January 1917

16
Triplane N5464 *DORIS* of Flt Sub-Lt Edward D
Crundall, 8 Naval Squadron, St-Eloi, France,
April 1917

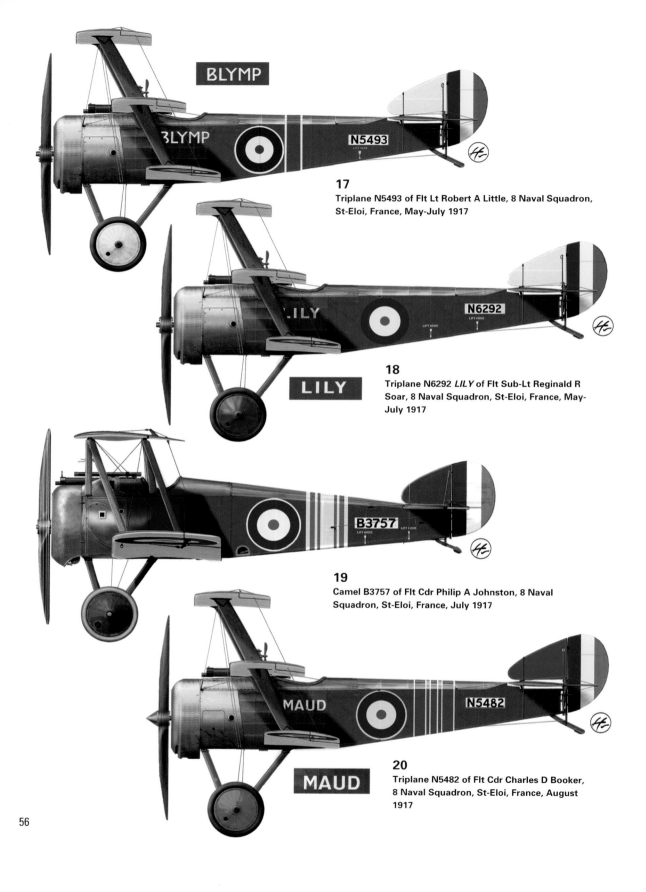

BLYMP

3LYMP N5493

17
Triplane N5493 of Flt Lt Robert A Little, 8 Naval Squadron, St-Eloi, France, May-July 1917

LILY N6292

LILY

18
Triplane N6292 *LILY* of Flt Sub-Lt Reginald R Soar, 8 Naval Squadron, St-Eloi, France, May-July 1917

B3757

19
Camel B3757 of Flt Cdr Philip A Johnston, 8 Naval Squadron, St-Eloi, France, July 1917

MAUD N5482

MAUD

20
Triplane N5482 of Flt Cdr Charles D Booker, 8 Naval Squadron, St-Eloi, France, August 1917

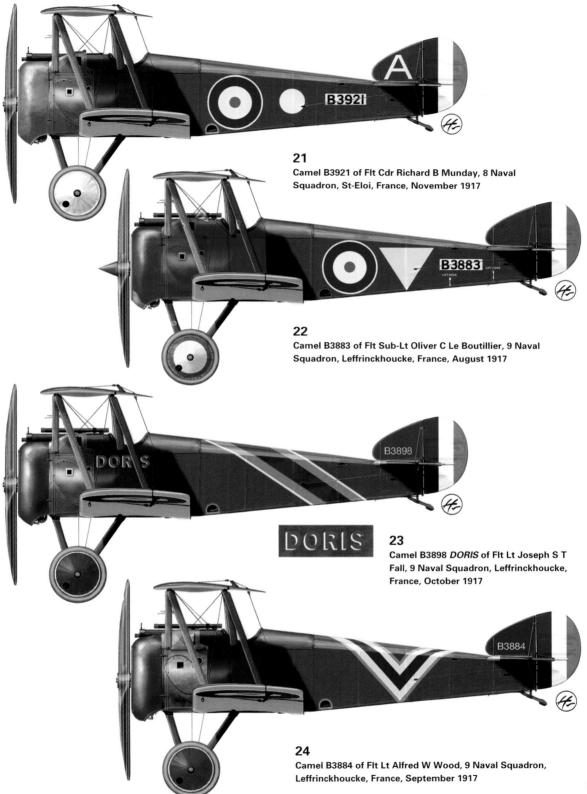

21
Camel B3921 of Flt Cdr Richard B Munday, 8 Naval Squadron, St-Eloi, France, November 1917

22
Camel B3883 of Flt Sub-Lt Oliver C Le Boutillier, 9 Naval Squadron, Leffrinckhoucke, France, August 1917

23
Camel B3898 *DORIS* of Flt Lt Joseph S T Fall, 9 Naval Squadron, Leffrinckhoucke, France, October 1917

24
Camel B3884 of Flt Lt Alfred W Wood, 9 Naval Squadron, Leffrinckhoucke, France, September 1917

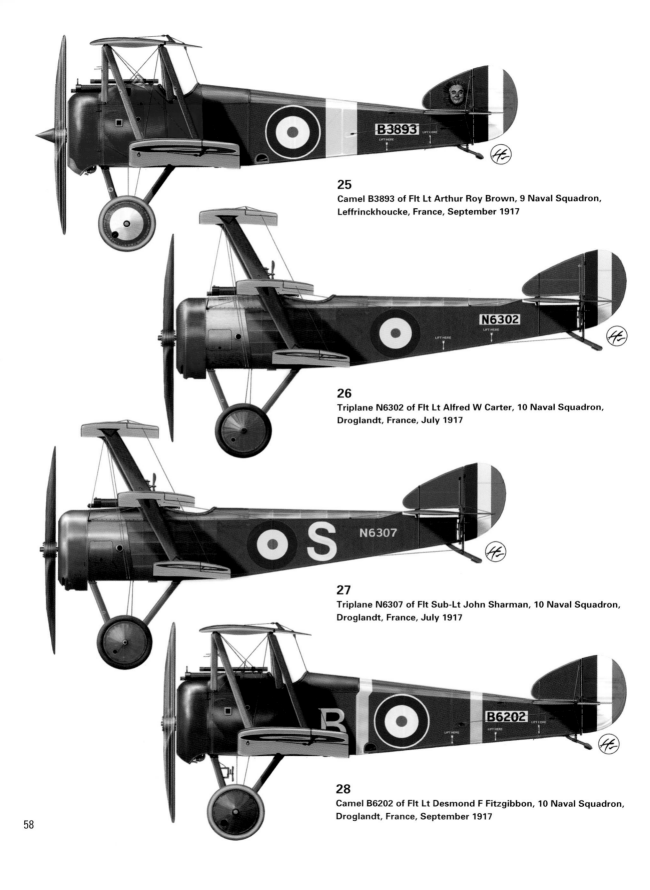

25
Camel B3893 of Flt Lt Arthur Roy Brown, 9 Naval Squadron, Leffrinckhoucke, France, September 1917

26
Triplane N6302 of Flt Lt Alfred W Carter, 10 Naval Squadron, Droglandt, France, July 1917

27
Triplane N6307 of Flt Sub-Lt John Sharman, 10 Naval Squadron, Droglandt, France, July 1917

28
Camel B6202 of Flt Lt Desmond F Fitzgibbon, 10 Naval Squadron, Droglandt, France, September 1917

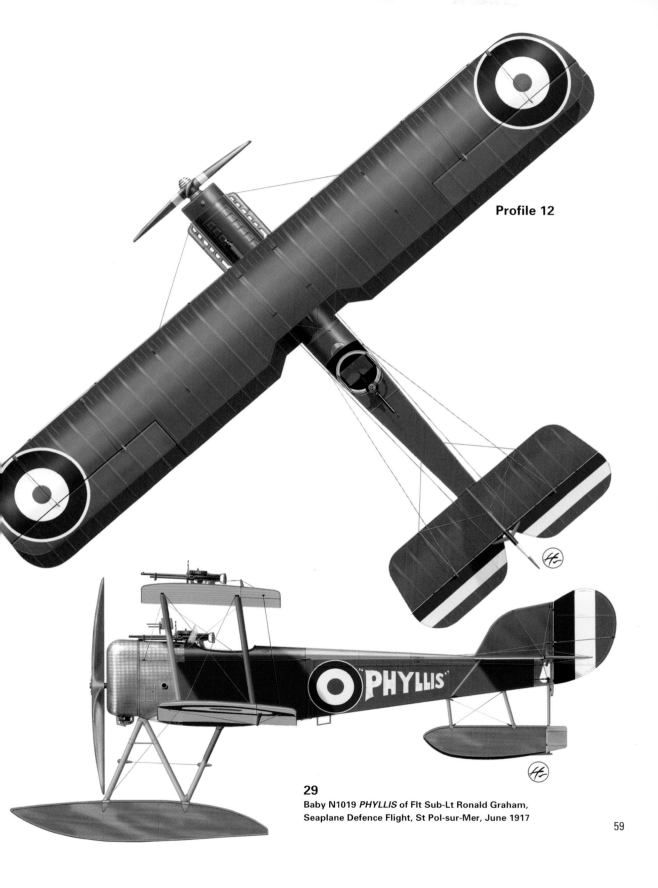

Profile 12

29
Baby N1019 *PHYLLIS* of Flt Sub-Lt Ronald Graham,
Seaplane Defence Flight, St Pol-sur-Mer, June 1917

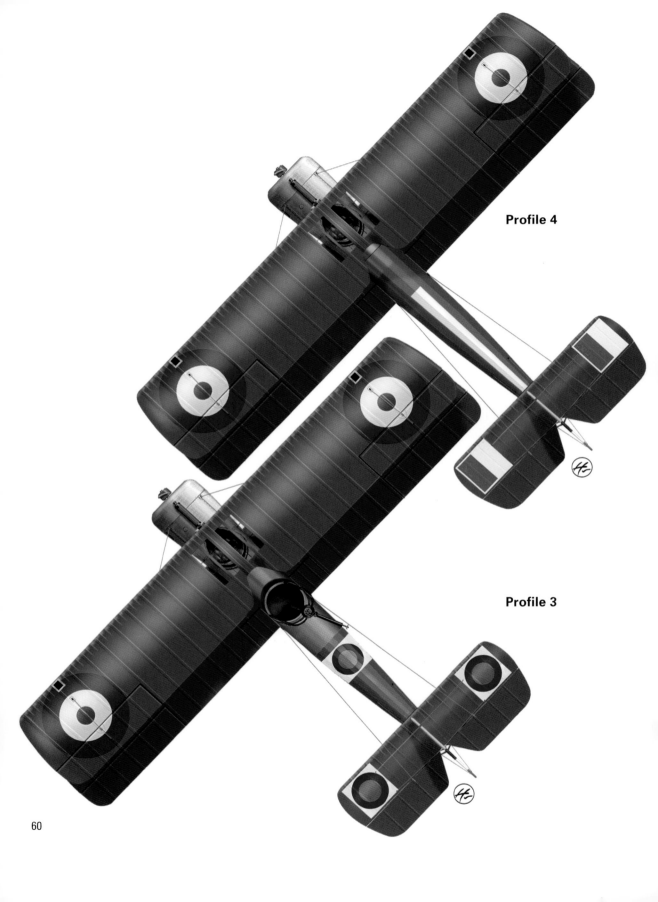

Profile 4

Profile 3

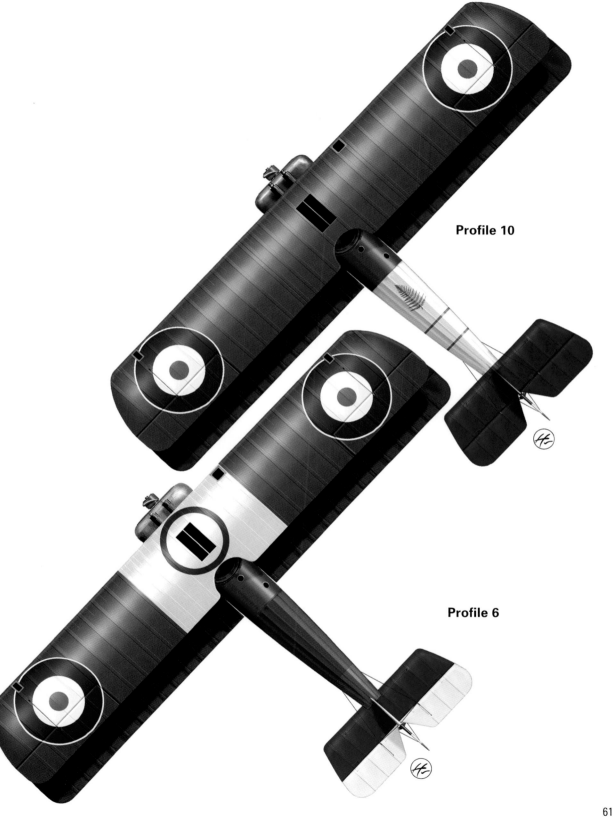

Profile 10

Profile 6

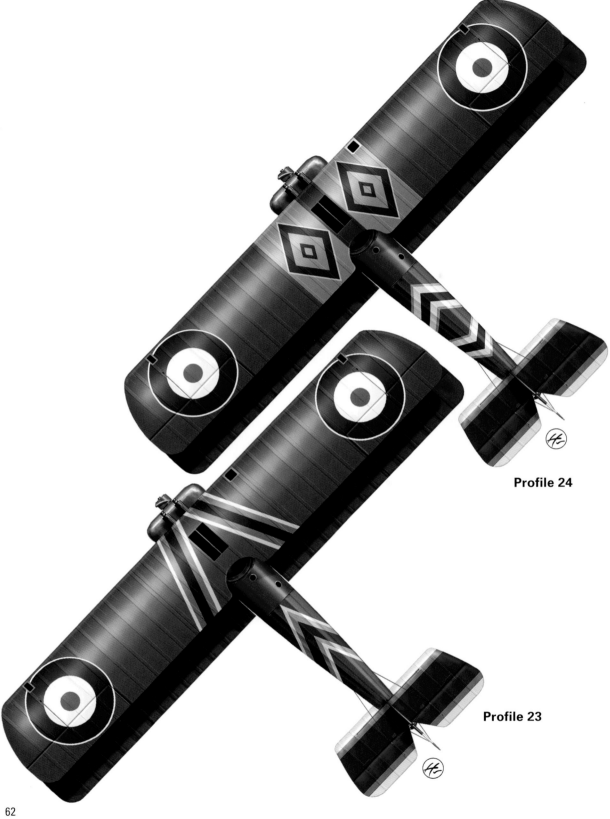

Profile 24

Profile 23

CAMELS VERSUS ALL COMERS

While the agonising succession of Allied offensives collectively called the Passchendaele campaign ground on, the Camel-equipped RNAS units continued to see action alongside their RFC and French allies. Attrition had been so heavy and replacements so difficult to find that 'Naval 6' was disbanded and its Camels and pilots meted out to 9 and 10 Naval Squadrons.

Flt Lt Munday of 'Naval 8' got September started with the first of several nocturnal balloon attacks, eliminating the enemy gasbag at Quiery la Motte at 2000 hrs on the 2nd. In a series of dogfights the following day, 'Naval 3' credited two D Vs to Lloyd Breadner and one to Flt Sub-Lt William Hargrove Chisam, a 22-year-old Scot from Carlisle.

On 3 September Flt Sub-Lt J E L Hunter of 'Naval 4' opened his account with a two-seater in concert with Flt Sub-Lt K V Turney. That same day the RNAS's deadliest duo of the month, Fall and Stackard of 'Naval 9', started off by sharing a D V with Flt Sub-Lts J E Scott and 19-year-old A W Wood from Heaton, West Yorkshire. Their victim was probably Flgmstr Brenner of MFJ I, who was wounded in the thigh. The next day Fall, Stackard and Scott downed a DFW. Those actions would typify the nature of 'Naval 9's' successes for the next few months.

Joe Fall, who had transferred into the squadron as a flight leader on 30 August, was a consummate pilot and a deadly fighter, but he also believed strongly in teamwork. Indeed, he made it a policy that would pervade not only his flight, but the whole squadron.

On 5 September Art Whealy, recently returned to 'Naval 3', downed a D V OOC northeast of Dixmude, as did Len Rochford and 'Kiwi' Beamish. That same day Roy Brown of 'Naval 9' teamed up with a hometown friend to down a two-seater OOC. Born on 13 February 1893, Stearne Tighe Edwards hailed from Carleton Place, where he had become firm friends with Brown and Murray Galbraith. After obtaining his certificate from the Aero Club of America on 13 October 1915, he had flown bombers with 3 Naval Wing, before rejoining Brown in 11, 6 and 9 Naval Squadrons. Also sharing in the victory were Flt Sub-Lts Banbury, Redgate and Wood.

On the 6th, 24-year-old Canadian Flt Sub-Lt Wilfred Austin Curtis from Havelock, Ontario, who had served in 'Naval 6' before being reassigned to 'Naval 10', sent a D V down OOC southeast of Dixmude. 'Naval 9's' Fall, Stackard, Scott, Wood and Flt Sub-Lt Hazel LeRoy Wallace, who was born in Earls Court, London, on 13 November 1897, claimed an Albatros two-seater that afternoon.

Flt Lt Ronald Francis Redpath was leading 'A' Flight of 'Naval 3' on 10 September when it caught a DFW of FA (A) 293b returning from a reconnaissance mission and brought it down between Furnes and

In 1916, Australian Flt Lt Richard Burnard Munday was a Curtiss JN-4 flight instructor at Cranwell, where his students included future ace Leonard H Rochford. The following year Munday joined Camel-equipped 'Naval 8' at St-Eloi, in France, and he was credited with the destruction of four aeroplanes and five kite balloons. He displayed a penchant for attacking the latter by night *(Norman Franks)*

Flt Lt Joe Fall of 'Naval 9' RNAS stands at right with his mechanics beside Camel B3898, in which he scored 11 victories between 3 September and 31 October 1917. For all his deadly skill, Fall was a believer in teamwork, as reflected in the fact that all of his successes in B3898 were shared with members of his flight (*Mike Westrop*)

A frequent member of Fall's team was Flt Sub-Lt Arthur R Wood, who scored seven victories in Camel B3884, which later bore the name *Dorothy*. All 11 of Wood's successes were shared with flight mates (*Mike Westrop*)

Rivalling anything at 'Naval 9' or 'Naval 10' for extravagance was Camel B6301 of 'Naval 3', assigned to Sqn Cdr Lloyd Breadner until he returned to Britain on 23 January 1918 and used thereafter by Flt Lt Len Rochford. Indeed, the latter was at the controls of B6301 when he shared in the downing of a DFW C V on 28 January 1918 and two Albatros D Vs 48 hours later (*Fleet Air Arm Museum JMB/GSL06337*)

Adinkerke, where Vfw Friedrich Eckhardt was captured. His wounded observer, Ltn Franz Adolf Gilge, died in hospital. Credit for this victory was shared by the whole flight, which consisted of Redpath, Anderson, Hayne and Flt Sub-Lt Gordon S Harrower.

On 11 September Christopher Draper of 'Naval 8' downed a D V OOC and Thornely scored his ninth victory (a two-seater) and subsequently received the DSC. Fall, Stackard and Wood of 'Naval 9' destroyed two D Vs, one in flames, over Leke, killing Ltn Friedrich von Götz of MFJ I. Also claiming his last success while escorting 'Naval 5' on a bombing sortie over the Bruges Docks that morning was Sqn Cdr Breadner, with a D V OOC, while Chisam claimed another and Rochford sent one down smoking. Returning to England on 23 January 1918, Breadner spent the rest of the war commanding the RAF's No 204 (training) Sqn with the rank of major. He subsequently served in the RCAF, rising to air chief marshal and Chief of the Air Staff in 1940. Lloyd Breadner died in Boston, Massachusetts, in 1953.

'Naval 10's' most significant success of the month occurred on 15 September when 'B' Flight was attacked by Albatros D Vs and a triplane. In the melee that followed, Flt Sub-Lt Norman Miers Macgregor, a 21-year-old Londoner with previous experience in 3 Naval Wing and four victories in 'Naval 6' prior to his transfer to 'Naval 10', fired into the triplane from a distance of 25 yards and saw it fall in a steep dive. Although credited under the usually dubious category of 'out of control,' Macgregor's claim matched a genuine enemy loss. Near Nachtigal the Germans found the body of *Jasta* 11's CO, Oblt Kurt Wolff, in the wreckage of F I 102/17 – the first, but by no means last, Fokker triplane to fall victim to a Camel.

On 16 September Flt Cdr Armstrong of 'Naval 3' downed two D Vs, while 'Naval 9's' Fall, Wallace and Wood despatched a DFW in flames over Mariakerke. Soon after that Wallace transferred to 'Naval 1'. Three days later yet another 'Naval 6' transferee to 'Naval 10' scored his first victory. Flt Sub-Lt Hugh Bingham Maund, who though born in Hampstead, London, on 31 May 1896 had seen action serving with the Canadian Expeditionary Force before joining the RNAS on 6 November 1916, claimed an Albatros destroyed east of Hooge.

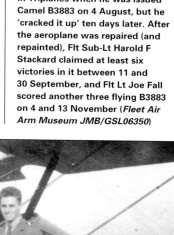

Below and bottom
Flt Sub-Lt Oliver C Le Boutillier, an American volunteer with 'Naval 9', had scored four victories in Triplanes when he was issued Camel B3883 on 4 August, but he 'cracked it up' ten days later. After the aeroplane was repaired (and repainted), Flt Sub-Lt Harold F Stackard claimed at least six victories in it between 11 and 30 September, and Flt Lt Joe Fall scored another three flying B3883 on 4 and 13 November (*Fleet Air Arm Museum JMB/GSL06350*)

An English member of 'Naval 10' from Hampstead, London, Hugh Bingham Maund scored two victories with the unit before it became No 210 Sqn RAF, followed by another nine thereafter until wounded in the hands on 28 May 1918 (*Mike Westrop*)

On 20 September the British launched an assault on the Menin Road Ridge. Aerial activity increased, both in the form of offensive patrols and low-level troop support and strafing missions. Manuel of 'Naval 10' destroyed a two-seater that day, while an Albatros D III fell OOC to a new member of 'Naval 9', 18-year-old Flt Sub-Lt Ronald Sykes from Stockton-on-Tees. Moments later, Sykes was shot down by Uffz Paul Bäumer of *Jasta* 'Boelcke', but he avoided capture and swam the Yser River to regain Allied lines. Later, with Nos 203 and 201 Sqns RAF, he raised his total to six.

'Naval 3' reported encountering 15 Albatros scouts in three formations on 23 September, and three D Vs were subsequently credited to Beamish and Harrower. The latter was wounded in the leg, however, and he may have been credited to Oblt Kurt von Döring of *Jasta* 4 despite making it back to Bray Dunes. Beamish, who would raise his total to 11 with No 203 Sqn RAF and be awarded the DSC, survived the war and returned to New Zealand, where he raised sheep and cattle until his death on 26 October 1986.

The 23rd also saw both Alexander, back at 'Naval 10' from Canadian leave, and Saint add OOCs to their respective tallies, as did Flt Sub-Lt Edward I Bussell. The latter's Camel was then downed in Allied lines, while Flt Sub-Lt 'Bill' Daly had to land his damaged aeroplane at 'Naval 4's' aerodrome. They were probably the 'Sopwiths' credited to Ltn d R Rudolf Wendelmuth and Oblt zur See Konrad Mettlich of *Jasta* 8. Edwards of 'Naval 9' downed two D Vs that same day, while 24-year-old Flt Sub-Lt J P Hales from Guelph, Ontario, was credited with one.

During a scrap over St Pierre Capelle on 24 September, Keirstead of 'Naval 4' claimed a D V OOC and another in flames. The latter was probably Oblt Werner Jahns of *Jasta* 28, who was killed that day.

'Naval 10's' Fitzgibbon and Daly each claimed D IIIs over Houthulst on the 26th, although the latter was wounded and possibly credited to Ltn Heinrich Bongartz of *Jasta* 36. Daly, with three victories, would score no more during World War 1, but joining Ray Collishaw in No 47 Sqn RAF during the Russian Civil War, he was credited with four Bolshevik aircraft destroyed in 1919 and awarded the DFC. Daly was killed four years later in a midair collision.

During a scrap northeast of Dixmude on 27 September, Curtis, Fitzgibbon and Flt Sub-Lt Stanley A Hamilton-Bowyer were credited with OOCs, but Flt Sub-Lt John S De Wilde, last seen lagging behind the formation, did not return. His was probably the Camel picked off by Vfw Ludwig Weber of *Jasta* 3. Posted to Home Establishment on 15 October, Fitzgibbon was awarded the DSC a month later.

The highlight of the 27th occurred when an audacious Albatros pilot crossed the lines and in quick succession shot down a British kite balloon and the RE 8 of No 9 Sqn that tried to defend it, followed by a second balloon. At that point the Albatros came under attack by Booker of 'Naval 8', who wounded the pilot in the arm and splintered his interplane struts before a British infantryman's bullet struck the Camel, forcing the ace to disengage. The German then turned on Booker, only to be hit in the engine by Thompson before he overshot the fighter in a vertical dive. As the enemy aviator tried to glide over the lines he was again attacked, this time by Nieuport pilot Lt John H Tudhope of No 40 Sqn RFC, and forced to land at Souchez. Albatros D V 2284/17 was given the captured serial G74 and its pilot, Oblt Hans Waldhausen of *Jasta* 37 (who had just scored his fourth, fifth and sixth victories), made a prisoner of war.

Booker was posted home for a rest in October, returning on 18 March 1918 to lead 'Naval 1' – which had been redesignated No 201 Sqn RAF by the time he scored his 24th victory on 15 May. Three successes on 13 August brought Maj Booker's total to 29, but later that same day he was killed by Ltn Ulrich Neckel of his longtime enemy, *Jasta* 12.

'Naval 10's' Trapp sent a D V crashing near Moorslede on 28 September, while 'Naval 9' pilots Edwards, Banbury, Redgate, Hales and 24-year-old Flt Sub-Lt Merril Samuel Taylor from Regina, Saskatchewan, claimed another. 'Sammy' Taylor went on to score six more victories with the redesignated No 209 Sqn RAF, before being killed on 7 July 1918 by Ltn Franz Büchner of *Jasta* 13.

Later on the 28th Flt Cdr Saint led six Camels to bomb Rumbeke aerodrome from 2000-3000 ft. Judging that altitude too high to be effective, Lt-Col F V Holt, commander of the RFC's No 22 Wing, ordered another, lower-level raid for 30 September. 'Naval 10's' pilots had been questioning the use of their Camels in the hazardous fighter-bomber role for some time, and now Sqn Cdr R F Redpath, recently transferred in from 'Naval 3' to serve as acting CO while Bell was away on sick leave, tried to postpone the mission. Finally, he flatly told Holt that 'his pilots weren't for it'.

After a personal consult with Redpath, who apparently based his conviction primarily on Saint's appraisal, Holt avoided issuing a formal order – realising the serious long-range consquences if it was refused – but subsequently passed this latest, and by no means first, instance of army-navy friction up the chain of command to Gen Trenchard. Although a strict disciplinarian, Trenchard, too, wished to avoid the morale-affecting appearance of mutiny, so he discretely transferred 'Naval 10' to Leffrinckhoucke, under the command of the 4th Brigade, on 5 October.

Until the move, Curtis claimed an Albatros on 1 October and a two-seater on the 15th. Saint downed a D V on the 20th for his seventh victory, before being transferred out of 'Naval 10' on the 26th to serve

Delivered from 'Naval 6' to 'Naval 10' on 30 August 1917, Camel B3882 was flown by Flt Sub-Lt George L Trapp, whose status as deputy leader of 'A' Flight was signified by only the foremost fuselage band extending over the upper decking. He was credited with an Albatros OOC on 9 September and another destroyed on the 28th for his fifth victory when at the controls of this machine. After scoring a sixth on 10 November, Trapp was killed in action three days later. His sister later married fellow Canadian ace Raymond Collishaw
(*Norman Franks*)

Four of five 'Naval 9' Camels at Leffrinckhoucke on 4 August 1917 sport a unique marking adopted by 'A' Flight – the head of comic actor George Robey, cut from an advertisement for his show *Zigzag*, pasted on the left side of the vertical stabiliser! Flt Lt Edmond Pierce flew B3881 in the foreground, although he scored no victories in it before returning to 'Naval 3'. The aeroplane behind it, B3893, was used by Flt Sub-Lt Arthur Roy Brown to down three enemy aircraft between 15 September and 13 October 1917, raising his tally to five and earning him a DSC (*Fleet Air Arm Museum JMB/GSL06356*)

as an instructor at Martlesham Heath. He had a varied postwar aviation career, holding Commercial Licence No 1, competing in air races and serving as a test pilot for the Royal Aircraft Factory, Gloster and the Royal Aircraft Establishment.

While 'Naval 10' lay relatively sidelined, 'Naval 8's' Flt Lt Munday burned a balloon at Brebières on 29 September and shared in the destruction of another with Draper on 3 October. Draper would score his ninth victory with No 208 Sqn on 8 May and then be awarded the DSC. Postwar, he penned an autobiography, *The Mad Major*, prior to his death on 16 January 1979.

'Naval 4's' Enstone downed a D V on 30 September, and the next day 20-year-old Flt Sub-Lt George Hatfield Dingley Gossip from Hampstead, North London, claimed a D V for his first victory.

'Naval 9's' aces continued to share their victories throughout September and October. One such team player, Mellersh, raised his total to five with No 209 Sqn in April 1918, and continued his RAF career through World War 2 to retire in 1951 as Sir Francis Mellersh. He was subsequently killed in a helicopter accident in May 1955.

'Naval 4' duelled *Jasta* 26 on the morning of 21 October, during which Keirstead downed two enemy aircraft. Shook claimed another, but was wounded, while Flt Sub-Lt E G A Eyre was killed by the *Staffelführer*, Oblt Bruno Loerzer. That afternoon, Fall and Wood of 'Naval 9' destroyed a two-seater in flames, while 'Naval 10's' Curtis, in concert with Flt Sub-Lts Harold L Nelson and Herbert J Emery, sent another aircraft down on fire near Dixmude, killing Vfw Max Häser and Uffz Kurt Busch of *Schutzstaffel* 16. A D V tried to attack Flt Sub-Lt Paynter, only to be shot down by Curtis and Emery.

On the 27th Stackard, Edwards, Banbury, Taylor and Redgate of 'Naval 9' claimed a D V over Slype. With Stackard's tally having now reached 15, this success completed his scoring. 'Naval 10's' Curtis and Flt Sub-Lt Kenneth V Stratton also shared in a D V that day, but Flt Sub-Lt George H Morang fell in flames to Ltn Heinrich Bongartz of *Jasta* 36. Brown of 'Naval 9' downed a D V on the 28th and Fall finished

October with a D V OOC on the 31st, probably wounding Uffz Kurt Reinhold of *Jasta* 24s.

In a change of pace from his usual modus operandi, Munday of 'Naval 8' destroyed a kite balloon at 0610 hrs on the morning of 7 November. Five days later Flt Lt George Trapp, now leading 'C' Flight of 'Naval 10', scored his sixth victory when he and Flt Sub-Lt Andrew G Beattie destroyed a two-seater. However, that afternoon, as Trapp was leading his flight in a diving attack on another two-seater, his Camel was seen to break up in the air and crash. While on leave, Ray Collishaw visited the Trapp family and ended up marrying George's sister, Neita.

On 13 November two Albatros two-seaters fell to Fall of 'Naval 9' – one of which was shared with Flt Sub-Lt Wood – and a third to Gossip. The latter subsequently claimed three more victories with No 204 Sqn RAF and left the unit with the rank of captain in August 1918. He died in 1922 and was buried in the Military Cemetery at Scutari, in Istanbul.

'Naval 1', finally equipped with Camels, reopened its account on 15 November with two D Vs credited to Kinkead and one to Findlay, who had transferred over since 'Naval 6's' dissolution. That day also saw Curtis of 'Naval 10' claim a D V, Manuel destroy another, Maund team up with Alexander to down a two-seater and Jack Hall, recovered from his wounding in May, requalified on Camels and reassigned to 'Naval 10', credited with a D V. Maund would score another six victories with his unit as No 210 Sqn RAF and take command of No 204 Sqn on 23 January 1919. For now, though, the RFC, in consequence of Sqn Cdr Redgate's undeclared act of 'mutiny' in September, officially terminated its association with 'Naval 10' on 20 November, placing it under the control of 4 Naval Wing, RNAS.

'Naval 9's' Redgate destroyed a D V on 20 November, and three days later Hickey and Tonks of 'Naval 4' each claimed a D V while 'Naval 9's' Banbury and Hales shared yet another D V. Hales would score his fifth victory on 11 August 1918 while with No 203 Sqn RAF, but he was killed by an AA shell 12 days thereafter. Tonks raised his tally to 12 after his unit became No 204 Sqn RAF, these successes earning him a DFC and Bar. On 14 July 1919 he was mortally wounded in an aeroplane crash.

Winter Interlude

Minifie of 'Naval 1' scored his first Camel victory (a D V) on 29 November. With the end of the German counteroffensive at Cambrai the next day, air activity tailed off, although the naval units bagged the occasional intruder and fought the odd dogfight throughout December.

A few new names joined those who scored during the winter months. On 5 December, 'Naval 8's' Compston teamed with Flt Sub-Lts Edward

Flt Lt Fred E Banbury of 'Naval 9' poses beside his Camel B6230 *RETA IV*, in which he scored five of his 11 victories between 28 September and 28 October 1917. Its fuselage band was red outlined in white, and the cowling and wheel hubs may also have been doped in red as well (*Norman Franks*)

Born in London on 6 May 1899, Edward Grahame Johnstone enlisted on his 18th birthday. After training with 'Naval 12', he was posted to 'Naval 8' in November, scored his first victory on 5 December and had raised his tally to ten all before his 19th birthday. Awarded the DSC, only Johnstone's youth kept him from a flight command. He finished the war with 17 victories to his name (*Norman Franks*)

Grahame Johnstone from London and Pruett Mullens Dennett from Southsea, Hampshire, to down a Rumpler OOC. Rosevear of 'Naval 1' destroyed a D V, while Irish-born Flt Cdr Guy William Price downed a D V and shared another OOC with 18-year-old Flt Sub-Lt Wilfred Henry Sneath from Hendon, North London.

Activity increased briefly on the 6th when Rosevear downed a two-seater and Ridley claimed a D V. 'Naval 8's' Kinkead was credited with both a two-seater and a D V destroyed, while Compston teamed up with Jordan and Dennett to despatch a DFW, after which Price and Day claimed a second and Compston, Jordan and Reid shared a third. Flt Cdr Rupert Winter, now with 'Naval 9', destroyed an Albatros two-seater with Flt Sub-Lt E M Knott, and Fall also claimed an Albatros two-seater, as well as a D V.

Two days later Minifie of 'Naval 1' destroyed a DFW, while Fall of 'Naval 9' despatched a D V northeast of the Houthulst Forest, probably killing Ltn Erich Daube of *Jasta* 'Boelcke'. On the 10th Macgregor and Flt Sub-Lt John G Clark of 'Naval 10' claimed an Albatros in flames, probably killing Ltn Herbert Wallner of *Jasta* 3. During another fight on 12 December an Albatros attacked Clark, and although Macgregor intervened and drove his assailant down OOC, Clark crashed behind enemy lines. He was taken prisoner as the eighth victory of Ltn Paul Billik, then serving in *Jasta* 7. With his score at seven, Macgregor was sent back to England on 28 January 1918 and awarded the DFC the following month.

On 22 December Flt Cdr Fall destroyed an Albatros two-seater for his 36th victory. This proved to be his final success for he was shipped home at the end of the month. Receiving two Bars to his DSC shortly afterwards, Joe Fall continued his RAF career until 1945 and then returned to Canada, where he died on 1 December 1988 in Enderby, British Columbia, aged 93.

The New Year was to bring a most unquiet spring to the Western Front as Germany, in the encouraging wake of the defeat of Romania, the Russian Revolution and the rout of the Italians at Caporetto, mobilised for an all-out offensive to knock France and Britain out of

Sharing in one of 'Naval 8's' earliest Camel victories on 13 July 1917, Flt Lt William Lancelot Jordan's score stood at eight by New Year's Day 1918. He had more than doubled it come the end of January, and Jordan eventually increased his total to 38 by 12 August (*N Franks*)

Displaying the bold stripes introduced by 'Naval 10's' groundcrews in December 1917 in an effort to boost morale, red and white striped Camel B6299, flown by Flt Lt Norman M Macgregor (now leading 'B' Flight, as signified by both fuselage bands extending over the upper decking), heads a lineup at Bray Dunes on 4 February 1918. B6204 behind it was flown by Flt Lt Walter G R Hinchliffe of 'C' Flight, who had destroyed an Albatros D V the day before this photograph was taken. He would down a two-seater on 10 March and eventually take his total to six after the unit had become No 210 Sqn RAF (*Fleet Air Arm Museum JMB/GSL06383*)

These five Camels, with black and white stripes, were assigned to 'Naval 10's' 'A' Flight at Teteghem shortly after Christmas 1917. Furthest from the camera is B6289, flown by Flt Sub-Lt Harold L Nelson, then B5663 of Flt Lt Wilfred A Curtis, B3869 of Flt Sub-Lt Sydney K F P Humphrey, B6320 of Flt Sub-Lt Frederick V Hall and B6225 of Flt Sub-Lt Kenneth V Stratton. The latter machine was transferred to Dover on 4 January 1918, having seen no combat in its new livery (*Mike Westrop*)

the war before the United States, which had joined the Allied cause on 6 April 1917, could fully deploy its forces on the Continent.

'Naval 8' ushered in the first day of 1918 with Flt Cdr Compston teaming up with Flt Sub-Lt Gerald Kempster Cooper and Capt Edward Mannock of No 40 Sqn RFC to bring a Hannover CL II down in Allied lines at Fampoux, killing Vfw Fritz Korbacher and Ltn Wilhelm Klein

Left and below
Fighters of *Jasta* 30 slipped past a 'C' Flight screen to attack 'B' Flight of 'Naval 10' on 3 January 1918, resulting in two more losses. Flt Sub-Lt Frank Booth was shot down and killed in red and white striped 'B' Flight Camel B5658 by Uffz Emil Liebert. Struck in the leg by Vfw Hans Oberländer, Flt Sub-Lt R A G Beattie of 'C' Flight lost lateral control upon landing and flipped his blue and white striped Camel N6351 over before being captured (*Andrew Kemp*)

of FA (A) 288b. Cooper, born on 13 November 1897 in Catford, south London, would score five more victories with No 208 Sqn.

Price downed a D V in flames on 2 January, killing Ltn Günther Auffarth of *Jasta* 29, while Compston got two DFWs the following day, the first of which, destroyed near Arras in concert with Jordan and Dennett, probably resulted in the deaths of Ltn d R Josef Lampart and Alexander Zipperer of FA 46b.

On 23 January Armstrong led an eight-aeroplane 'Naval 3' patrol that encountered four DFWs escorted by three 'Scouts new type' over the Houthulst Forest. Flt Lt Anderson achieved acedom at long last when he despatched a DFW, but Flt Sub-Lt Herbert S J E Youens was lost – claimed by Ltn d R Carl Degelow of *Jasta* 7, but credited, through an official mix-up, to Ltn Gustav Wandelt of *Jasta* 36. Five minutes later *Jasta* 36 ran into 'Naval 10's' Camels over Staden, resulting in another two-seater 'destroyed' by Curtis and a D V credited to Alexander, who was back from leave and leading 'C' Flight. Once again a Camel was lost,

Camel B5663 was flown by Flt Lt Wilfred A Curtis when he led 'Naval 10's' 'A' Flight, as indicated by both white bars extending over the fuselage's upper decking. Curtis was flying this aircraft when he and Flt Sub-Lt Frederick C Hall destroyed an Albatros D V on 5 December 1917 (*Stuart Taylor*)

On 23 January 1918 'Naval 10's' Curtis scored his 13th victory (a two-seater near Staden) in B6450, while squadronmate Flt Sub-Lt Ross A Blyth was killed in B5663 when he was involved in a mid-air collision with an Albatros D Va flown by Ltn Gustav Wandelt of *Jasta* 36. The latter also perished (*Andrew Kemp*)

this time in a midair collision that killed Flt Sub-Lt Ross A Blyth and his opponent, Ltn Wandelt.

Leaving 10 Naval Squadron on 27 January with 13 victories, Wilfred Curtis was awarded the DSC and Bar. During World War 2 he rose to the rank of air marshal in the RCAF and became its Chief of Air Staff in 1947. Retiring in 1953, Curtis died on 7 August 1977.

'Naval 8's' team effort continued on the 24th when Price claimed a D V destroyed and two fell OOC to Jordan and Johnstone. The latter pair shared one of their successes with Flt Sub-Lt Reginald Leach Johns, a 23-year-old pilot from Kilburn in northwest London. Also destroying a D V was Flt Sub-Lt James Butler White, a 24-year-old Canadian from Manitoulin Island, Ontario. One of their victims, Uffz Fritz Jacob of *Jasta* 12, came down at Izel mortally wounded.

Jordan and Johnstone claimed a Pfalz destroyed near Beaumont on 25 January. This may have been Ltn d R Ernst Paland, who was wounded just four days after joining *Jasta* 20. On the 28th, Price downed a two-seater in flames, killing Gefrs Wilhelm Walter and Ludwig Neeb of *Schusta* 17.

On 2 February 'Naval 8's' Compston, Day and Johns collaborated in driving down a D V and a DFW, while White claimed a second D V OOC. With four to his name at that point, Johns would raise his score to nine victories with No 208 Sqn prior to being killed in a flying accident on 11 July 1918. White added ten more to his two while with the same unit, and became a stockbroker after the war. He passed away on 2 January 1972.

Edwards and Redgate of 'Naval 9' destroyed an Albatros two-seater on the morning of 3 February. It was Redgate's tenth victory, to which he would add six more after his unit became No 209 Sqn, and Edwards' eighth of 11 before he too was killed in a flying accident – tragically, the day after the armistice, 12 November 1918.

Munday of 'Naval 8' downed a D V at 1230 hrs on 3 February. Ninety minutes later 'Naval 9' had its first of many encounters with the Fokker Dr I, which had recently been delivered to the Germans' leading *Staffeln* for the coming offensive. During the course of the fight, Flt Lt Winter and Flt Sub-Lt M A Harker were credited with destroying a triplane, but moments later Winter's wings folded and he crashed to his death. Although he was the only casualty in the fight, 'Naval 9's' opponent, *Jasta* 26, managed to outclaim the British this time by crediting a single Camel to Offz Stv Otto Fruhner and three to Offz Stv Otto Esswein.

The 3rd also saw Flt Sub-Lt Walter George Raymond score his first success with a D V destroyed southwest of Rumbeke. Born in Liverpool on 10 June 1894, he had served in the Royal Artillery prior to joining the RNAS in 1916 and spending time as an instructor at Cranwell. Raymond was eventually transferred to 'Naval 10' in January 1918.

A Dr I OOC was credited to Flt Sub-Lt Ronald Cory Berlyn on 5 February. Born in Birmingham on 16 February 1899, Berlyn had been in 4 and 12 Naval Squadrons before joining 'Naval 3' in January. Also on the 5th, Flt Ldr McDonald of 'Naval 8' teamed up with Day, Sneath and Flt Lt Herbert Howland Snowdon Fowler to destroy a D V. Having claimed his 11th victory, Day was diving on another D V when his

Flt Lt Rupert R Winter, who had flown Nieuports with 'Naval 6' and Camels with 'Naval 9', finally attained ace status on 3 February 1918 when he shared his fifth victory (a Fokker Dr I) with Flt Sub-Lt M A Harker. Moments later, however, his Camel, B6430, broke up in the air. He was the only fatality in the dogfight, which saw *Jasta* 26 lose no men and its own pilots over-claim by three (*Mike Westrop*)

Camel broke up and he was killed. His demise was credited to Ltn Günther Schuster of *Jasta* 29.

Roderick McDonald would share in one more victory, his eighth, with No 208 Sqn on 21 April. On 8 May, however, he was killed by Vfw Julius Trotsky of *Jasta* 43.

On 16 February Price, Fowler and Sneath claimed a D V in flames over Pronville. Staying on with No 208 Sqn, Sneath would share his fifth victory (a Fokker Dr I) with Teddy Gerrard and G K Cooper on 6 April, but he was shot down in flames shortly thereafter by Ltn d R Karl Hertz of *Jasta* 59. Herb Fowler would raise his score to six with No 208 Sqn, and having survived the war he eventually died of a heart attack on 26 January 1962.

On 18 February Guy Price, whose score stood at 12, was engaged in a low-level strafing mission when his flight was jumped by *Jasta* 23b, resulting in he and Flt Sub-Lt C R Walworth being killed by Ltn Theodor Rumpel and Vfw Heinrich Küllmer. That same morning Jordan of 'Naval 8' downed a D V for his 18th victory, to which he would add 21 more with No 208 Sqn and survive the war, only to die in a car accident in 1930. Another D V fell to Compston for his 25th, and last, victory before going home on rest. Awarded the DSO, DSC and two Bars, Maj Compston would command No 40 Sqn in August 1918 and serve in the RAF again in World War 2. He died on 28 January 1962.

Flt Lt J G Manuel, now leading 'Naval 10's' B Flight, and Flt Sub-Lt Hall each downed a D V on the 18th, but Flt Sub-Lt Ronald E Burr was shot down in Allied lines by Oblt Bruno Loerzer of *Jasta* 26. He subsequently died of his injuries. Fred Hall's score stood at four, and he would add three more as a lieutenant in No 210 Sqn before being killed on 15 May when Lt Magnus Kelly's Camel was hit by an AA shell that in turn caused it to career into Hall's aeroplane.

On 19 February Flt Lt A W Carter, back at 'Naval 10' following his Canadian leave, shared credit with Flt Lt Rosevear of 'Naval 1' for sending Albatros D Va 4495/17 crashing into the Ypres-Comines canal south of Zillebeke. Its pilot, Ltn Hans von Puttkammer of *Jasta* 3, was captured.

Nick Carter scored seven more victories after his unit became No 210 Sqn and remained in RAF service until 1953, retiring as an air marshal, an Officer of the Order of the British Empire and a Member of the Order of the British Empire. Although practically blind in later years, that did not stop him from attending the last World War 1 aces' reunion in Paris in November 1981, where he met his old 'Naval 3' squadronmate Len Rochford. Carter died in Vancouver on 17 December 1986.

On 21 February Richard Munday of 'Naval 8' downed a two-seater for his ninth victory. Awarded the DSC, he ended the war with the rank of major serving in the RAF.

Flt Lt Harold T Mellings, who had scored five victories in the eastern Mediterranean with 2 Naval Wing before joining 'Naval 10' on 17 February, finished the month with a D V on the 28th.

As the RNAS pilots girded themselves for March, with its return of spring and its attendant increase in air activity, few realised that their own air arm was entering its last month of existence as such.

John Gerald Manuel, who hailed from Winnipeg, Manitoba, was credited with seven victories while serving with 'Naval 10' and another six with No 210 Sqn RAF (*Mike Westrop*)

SEAPLANE DEFENCE AND BOMBER ACES

Serving alongside the regular fighter units in Flanders was the Seaplane Defence Flight (SDF). Formed at St Pol in June 1917 with a mixed bag of Sopwith Baby floatplanes and Pups, its duties including escorting Allied seaplanes and attacking enemy aircraft along the coast. The SDF soon saw action. On the 19th two Babies were escorting a Short 184 when they were attacked by three floatplanes from German *Seeflugstaffel* II north-northeast of Nieuport. Two British floatplanes were lost, but Flt Sub-Lt Ronald Graham, in Baby N1019, downed one of the Germans, then landed alongside a French destroyer and directed it to assist the casualties on both sides. One of his victims, Ltn d R Walter Dyck, died of wounds soon after.

Born in Yokohama, Japan, on 19 July 1896, Ronnie Graham was a medical student when war broke out, and he joined the RNAS in September 1915. While with the SDF, Graham marked his Baby with the name *Phyllis* after his girlfriend, Nurse Phyllis Farmer. Put in command of the flight on 30 June 1917, he was flying Pup N6478 when he and Flt Sub-Lts Leonard H Slatter and L P Fisher shot down Friedrichshafen FF 33l 1246 on 12 August, killing Flgmstr Walter Paatz and Vfw Heinrich Putz of *Seeflugstaffel* I.

Leonard Horatio Slatter, born on 8 December 1894 and educated in South Africa, was a civil engineer before the war and then a despatch rider in an armoured car unit prior to joining the RNAS as an observer in 1916. After more than 100 flying hours in Short floatplanes, he took pilot training in July. Following a spell flying in two-seaters, Slatter was assigned to the SDF in July.

In September, the SDF received its first Camels, and on the 15th of the month Graham teamed up with Slatter to destroy an Albatros W 4 in flames, killing Flgmstr Fritz Dyke of *Seeflugstaffel* I. Ten days later

Maj Ronald Graham began his fighting career with the SDF, scoring his first victory in a Sopwith Baby and his last in a Camel as commander of the flight's final wartime incarnation, No 213 Sqn RAF (*Norman Franks*)

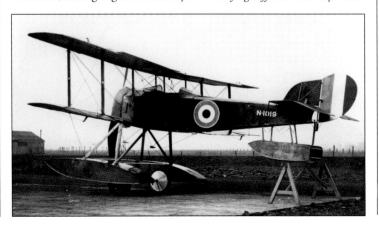

Flt Sub-Lt Graham's Blackburn-built Sopwith Baby N1019, which had sported the name of his girlfriend Phyllis on the fuselage side, is shown sometime after July 1917, when its armament was removed and a white surround added to the cockades. Graham scored his first victory in another Baby, N1016, on 19 June 1917 (*Fleet Air Arm Museum JMB/GSL05649*)

Graham and Slatter were each credited with a floatplane. One of these was FF 33l 1582 of *Seeflugstaffel* I, which crashed near Ostend with Vzflgm Plattenburg wounded and Ltn Brettmann unhurt. Slatter also shot down an Albatros D III on 27 October.

On 13 November 19-year-old Londoner Flt Sub-Lt Colin Peter Brown teamed up with two other pilots to down a D V, to which he would add 13 more victories after his unit became No 213 Sqn RAF. Continuing his postwar career with the RAF, Colin Brown retired from the Air Ministry as an air vice-marshal and a CBE. He eventually died on 19 October 1965.

Ray Collishaw assumed command of the SDF on 23 November. On 4 December Flt Sub-Lt John Pinder, recently transferred in from 'Naval 9', shared in the destruction of a two-seater with 19-year-old Flt Sub-Lt George Chisholme MacKay from Toronto. The next day Pinder and MacKay teamed up with Dublin-born, York-educated Flt Sub-Lt Maurice Lea Cooper and John de Champbourne Paynter, from Chelsea, Hampshire, to destroy an Albatros two-seater northwest of Wenduyne.

On 10 December Collishaw claimed a two-seater 'driven down' (a dubious victory at that point in the war) and nine days later he was credited with an Albatros D V OOC and MacKay a two-seater OOC.

In January 1918 the SDF, expanded to squadron strength and fully equipped with Camels, was redesignated 13 Naval Squadron. On 3 January Flt Cdr M G Day, a 21-year-old from St Ives, Huntingdonshire, whose previous experience included test flying on the Isle of Grain, downed a two-seater OOC, and he would similarly claim a Dr I over Staden on the 25th. Four days later Slatter teamed up with Flt Sub-Lts Cooper and J E Greene from Winnipeg to destroy a floatplane off Blankenberghe Pier. The next day Paynter and Day downed a two-seater. On 19 February, Day, Bell, Paynter, Flt Sub-Lt J C Stovin and G D Smith sent a floatplane down in flames east of Ostend.

At that point Day had scored five victories in six weeks. On 27 February his flight encountered six floatplanes and he raced ahead, aiming to break up the formation before his less experienced wingmen reached it. However, he was driven into the sea in flames 25 miles west of Dunkirk by the floatplane crew of Flgmstr Dreyer and Ltn Frantz of Ostend-based *Seeflugstation* II. Day was last seen clinging to the wreckage of his Camel, N6363, but by the time a destroyer arrived he was gone.

Slatter downed a D V on 11 March. The next day, Cooper, Greene, MacKay and Flt Sub-Lt E V Bell despatched a Rumpler in flames. During a coastal run-in with *Seefront Staffel* II on 24 March, Flt Sub-Lt F C Messiter was shot down by Flgmstr Christian Kairies, although he was soon rescued. Kairies was in turn wounded when his Pfalz D IIIa was shot down by MacKay east of Middelkerke, and Greene claimed another Pfalz.

On 1 April the squadron claimed three floatplanes that were credited to Cooper, Greene and MacKay. *Seeflugstaffel* I actually lost two, resulting

Flt Cdr Leonard H Slatter in the cockpit of his Pup N6203 *"MINA"* while serving in the SDF in July 1917. He also added the initial 'S' on the fuselage upper decking just above the roundel (*Norman Franks*)

After being injured in a Nieuport crash with 'Naval 6' on 6 April 1917 and sharing in a victory with 'Naval 9' on 27 October that same year, Flt Lt John de Campbourne Paynter came into his own flying Camels with 'Naval 13' in 1918, scoring three victories before it became No 213 Sqn RAF and another five thereafter. He was killed during a German air raid on Bergues airfield on the night of 18 June 1918 (*Mike Westrop*)

in the deaths of Flgmstr Hermann Behrendt, Ltn zur See Georg Hauptvogel, Flgmstr Bruno Fricke and Ltn zur See Walter Tornau. At that point 13 Naval Squadron became No 213 Sqn RAF, and Cooper, Greene, MacKay and Paynter would add additional victories to their tallies with this unit – as would several more aces, including the US Navy's Lt(jg) David S Ingalls, who scored six victories while attached to No 213 Sqn.

Capt John Paynter, who was promoted to flight commander during the spring, had increased his tally to ten victories by the time he was killed during a German air raid on No 213 Sqn's airfield at Bergues on the night of 18 June. The ace had failed to take shelter and he was killed by bomb fragments. Fellow ace Capt Maurice Cooper also perished before war's end, being lost to ground fire while bombing a train northeast of Gitsberg on 2 October. Awarded the DFC, Capt Greene shared in the destruction of a Fokker D VII (his 15th victory) with US Navy Lt Kenneth MacLeish on 14 October. Both men were killed later that same day, however, their aircraft being two of the six No 213 Sqn Camels downed by MFJ IV for the loss of Ltn zur See Max Stinsky.

Awarded the DSC and Bar, Slatter left No 213 Sqn in July to serve as an instructor in the 4th Air Depot. Nevertheless, on 30 August he slipped over the lines to shoot down a Halberstadt two-seater, for which he was awarded the DFC. Serving in No 47 Sqn in South Russia in 1919, he continued his RAF career through World War 2, rising to the position of commander-in-chief, Coastal Command, with the rank of air marshal, in 1945. Awarded the OBE, Slatter died in 1961.

After recovering from a crash suffered on 29 December 1917 – while stunting for Miss Farmer – Maj Graham returned to command No 213 Sqn in May 1918 and scored his fifth victory over an LVG on 19 October. Awarded the DSO, DSC and Bar and the DFC, as well as the CdG and Belgian Order of the Crown, Graham celebrated war's end by marrying Phyllis at Reshail Church on 30 November. He retired from the RAF on 29 June 1948 as an air vice-marshal, CB, CBE, and died at Sannox, Isle of Arran, Scotland, on 23 June 1967.

BOMBER ACES

Less celebrated than the fighter aces were the bomber crewmen, who, in the course of daily missions in and out of harm's way, managed not only to survive but to amass multiple enemy aircraft to their credit. In the case of the RNAS, virtually all of its bombing aces came from 'Naval 5'.

On 31 December 1916, 'B' Naval Squadron of 5 Naval Wing was redesignated 5 Naval Squadron, and it flew night bombing missions against coastal aerodromes and other installations from Coudequerque. Initially operating Sopwith 1½ Strutters, the unit moved to Petite Synthe on 1 April 1917 and began to re-equip with DH 4s the following month. On 17 July its CO, Sqn Cdr E T Newton Clare, was replaced by fighter ace Stanley Goble.

Among the unit's most seasoned veterans, Charles Philip Oldfield Bartlett was born in Weston-super-Mare, Somerset, on 3 January 1889, the son of Canon Bartlett, the rector of Willsersley and later vicar of Minsterworth, Gloucestershire. In 1916 Bartlett enlisted in the RNAS and earned Royal Aero Club Certificate No 3118 on 21 June. He went

Born in Weston-super-Mare, Somerset, on 3 January 1889, Charles Philip Oldfield Bartlett flew 101 bombing sorties in Sopwith 1½ Strutters and DH 4s with 'Naval 5' and its later RAF incarnation, No 205 Sqn. He was credited with eight victories, awarded the DSC and Bar and wrote a memoir, *Bomber Pilot 1916-1918*, before his death at the age of 97 (*Norman Franks*)

T F Le Mesurier, wearing a 'Flotation Waistcoat' over his leather flying jacket – a common addition to an RNAS airman's flight kit for missions over or near the sea – chats with C P O Bartlett and Flt Sub-Lt Garrett prior to taking off on a raid from Petite Synthe in 1917 (*Norman Franks*)

on to complete 101 sorties with 'Naval 5' and its later RAF incarnation, No 205 Sqn, being credited with eight victories and receiving the DSC and Bar.

'By the beginning of July we mustered five DH 4s, and we were able to carry out a number of effective day missions', Bartlett wrote in his memoir, *Bomber Pilot, 1916-1918*. 'The DH 4 was well adapted for bomber work, capable of carrying a 450-lb bomb load and, with an observer or gunlayer in the back handling twin Lewis guns on a Scarff mounting, it had good protection. The pilot had twin synchronised Vickers guns firing forward through the propeller arc.

'Originally fitted with a 250 hp Rolls Royce Eagle VI engine, later models had the 275 hp Eagle VII and, finally, the 375 hp Eagle VIII, the last giving a top speed of around 130 knots and a ceiling of some 22,000 ft. Our early DH 4s, however, hardly exceeded 110 knots, and we had difficulty in getting them above 15,000 ft with bombs, but they handled well and the Rolls-Eagle VI proved wonderfully reliable. An effective bombsight enabled precision bombing to be carried out by the observer or gunlayer, who steered the pilot over the target by means of string "reins". This was the only means of communication between the rear man and the pilot.'

Much younger than Bartlett, but equally as skilled, was Thomas Frederick Le Mesurier, born in Merton Park, Surrey, on 16 February 1897 and educated at Rutlish School and Hurstpierpoint College. Joining the RNAS on 23 July 1915, he had risen to the rank of flight lieutenant by the end of 1916 and was made a flight leader at 'Naval 5' in June 1917. During a raid on Bruges on 3 June, Le Mesurier and his observer, Flt Sub-Lt R G St John, were credited with driving an attacking Albatros D III down OOC.

Bartlett was flying DH 4 N5967 with AGL S D Sambrook on a strike on the Bruges docks when they were attacked by Albatros D Vs. 'We were forced to drop our bombs and fight a rearguard action', Bartlett recalled. 'Fortunately, our formation was good and close so that none ventured to dive down into our midst. Sambrook, my gunlayer, put up good shooting, and one that attacked us went down in a vertical nose dive but we were unable to follow him as a second took his place and needed all Sambrook's attention'. The D V was credited to both crewmen as OOC.

Attacking Snellegem aerodrome on 5 August, Le Mesurier and AGL H S Jackson were credited with two D Vs. 'Le Mesurier has been awarded a Bar to his DSC – damn well deserved', Bartlett noted a few days later. Le Mesurier and Jackson downed another D V OOC on 19 August and again on 11 September, the latter over Sparappelhoek aerodrome. 'Le Mesurier was attacked by a scout who put an explosive bullet into the Lewis trays behind the observer's seat and set off some of the ammunition', Bartlett wrote of the latter occasion, 'The trays probably saved the gunlayer, who accounted for the scout'.

On 28 September Flt Lt Charles Roger Lupton and his observer, AGL L G Smith, downed a D V OOC. Born in Roundhay, Leeds, on 27 January 1898, 'Luppy' Lupton had joined the RNAS in July 1916.

Le Mesurier and Jackson scored again on 15 and 21 October, the latter date also seeing a D V credited to Flt Sub-Lt A Shaw and AGL Walter

Naylor. Later assigned to 'Naval 11', which subsequently became No 211 Sqn RAF, Flt Cdr Le Mesurier had received a second Bar to his DSC by 29 May 1918 when his DH 9 was hit by AA fire over Pervyse and broke up 20 ft above Allied lines. Both Le Mesurier and his observer, 2Lt R Lardner, were fatally wounded when their aircraft struck the ground.

On 4 November 1917 Shaw and Naylor downed a D V over Engel aerodrome. A sortie to Aertrycke on 8 December saw a few more DH 4 aces claim their first successes as Flt Lt Euan Dickson and Naylor drove a D V down at 1140 hrs and Flt Sub-Lt John Gamon and AGL Winter, in concert with Lupton and Smith, accounted for another ten minutes later.

Born in Sheffield on 31 March 1892, Dickson had emigrated to New Zealand in 1912, where he worked as an engineer, but returned to England in 1914 and joined the RNAS on 30 July 1916. After getting his flying certificate on 12 December 1916, he was posted to 'Naval 10' on 31 March 1917. However, after a series of accidents he was 'washed out' of the squadron on 29 April and transferred to 'Naval 5'. There, he would find success – and, ironically, acedom – as a bomber pilot, starting with the award of the DSC on 16 November.

John Gamon was born in Parkgate, Cheshire, on 25 July 1898, and he joined the RNAS five days after his 18th birthday. Assigned to 'Naval 4' on 14 July, he became lost in sea mist on the 24th and ditched his Camel off Calais. He too was transferred to 'Naval 5', joining the unit on 18 August.

On 30 January 1918, 'Naval 5' bombed Oostcamp aerodrome. 'Immediately after dropping we were heavily engaged by some 15 to 20 enemy aircraft that seemed to appear suddenly from nowhere, diving down out of the sun and choosing their attack when our formation was split up after dropping and had not had time to reform', Bartlett recalled. 'I found three of them on my tail, and a fourth came in head-on. I had to zoom to avoid him and never had time to use my front guns, but he did, shooting below my port wing prior to joining the other three on my tail. At the same time my engine cut out on three cylinders and my revs dropped away to 1300'.

This photograph of personnel from 'Naval 5' includes, front row, from left to right, R G St John, unknown, Wallace Newton-Clare (third from left), Thomas F Le Mesurier (seven victories), Stanley J Goble (ten victories), I N C Clarke, Robert Jope-Slade and C P O Bartlett (eight victories). Charles R Lupton (standing, sixth from left) scored five victories and Euan Dickson (second from right) was credited with 14 (*Norman Franks*)

DH 5 N6000 was C P O Bartlett's favourite aeroplane, but several other aces with 'Naval 5' scored while crewing it. The machine also boasted an extraordinarily extravagant colour scheme for a bomber, with tricolour elevators and a lot of red over the nose, fuselage and tail (*Fleet Air Arm Museum JMB/GSL02918*)

The radiator was also hit, but Naylor managed to claim one of their pursuers in flames, compelling the other three to hold back. Somehow Bartlett made it over the lines, remarking 'I actually managed to land at the aerodrome with my radiator empty and my engine so hot that our fitters could not get near it – why it never seized is a miracle. A bullet had severed the induction port feeding the front three starboard cylinders and another one had made a mess of the radiator. It speaks volumes for the old Rolls-Royce Eagle VII engine'.

Dickson and Naylor scored victories on 17 and 18 February. On 16 March Bartlett led eight bombers to the aerodrome and ammunition dump at Busigny, during which Dickson and Flt Sub-Lt W H Scott destroyed a D V. Sqn Cdr Goble, along as observer to Flt Lt Toby Watkins, was credited with two D Vs, bringing his total to ten.

On 18 March 'Naval 5' was involved in a multi-squadron operation that ran afoul of JG I, resulting in nine German claims, including the DH 4 of Flt Sub-Lt R B Ransford and AGL L G Smith, killed by Hptm Wilhelm Reinhard of *Jasta* 6. 'I had my front guns onto an Albatros at about 30 yards range for a few seconds as he cut across our bows', Bartlett wrote, 'and got some 20-30 rounds into him, but he dived, coming up again under our tail. I slewed enough for Naylor to get a long burst into him, and he went down pouring black smoke from his tail'. Dickson and Scott were also credited with an Albatros OOC.

A front view of DH 4 N6000, bombed-up for a mission and displaying its red engine cowling and white and red striped propeller spinner (*Fleet Air Arm Museum JMB/GSL021919*)

The German offensive on 21 March 1918 brought 'Naval 5's' activities to a climax. That first day started with a move to Champien aerodrome and several bombing sorties. During one of the latter Bartlett and Naylor claimed a triplane OOC. Lupton and 19-year-old AGL Albert George Wood downed a D V the following day. During an attack on the Somme bridges on 27 March, Bartlett and Naylor holed a kite balloon (which was pulled down), strafed soldiers and sent 'a long burst into a grey and green Albatros just below us and saw him crash in a field'. Dickson and Scott were credited with another Albatros near Raincourt.

Again approaching Raincourt on the 28th, Bartlett's DH came under attack by eight enemy aeroplanes. 'I dived on a yellow Pfalz and drove him down' he wrote. 'It then being altogether too hot, I made for the lines, leaving it to Naylor. He got one of the remaining seven down out of control, and two Fokker triplanes converging on our tail collided and went down locked together, bursting into flames on the ground. Diving at 180 mph, we outpaced the remaining triplane and three Halberstadts and crossed the lines'. Although German records do not describe any losses that match his description, Bartlett was credited with three Dr Is, bringing his total to eight. Dickson and Flt Sub-Lt Stewart were credited with a Pfalz. That afternoon 'Naval 5' resettled at Yvrench aerodrome.

Gamon and Lt R Scott downed a Dr I on 30 March. Two days later, 'Naval 5' became No 205 Sqn RAF, in which Dickson and Naylor brought their scores up to 14 and Gamon raised his to seven. Dickson, who survived 180 missions, returned to New Zealand, where he pursued careers in civil aviation and engineering, retiring as chairman of the Eden Motor Co in 1964 and dying in Auckland on 10 March 1980.

Lupton and Wood were credited with a Dr I in flames on 6 April and a Pfalz D IIIa the next day. Lupton flew more than 60 missions and was awarded the DSC and Bar, but he and Wood were killed in action on 9 May 1918, both being buried at Vignacourt.

John Gamon fainted after being wounded by an AA hit on 17 June 1918, but his observer happened to be Goble, who, being a qualified pilot, took over the controls, pulled their DH 4 out of its dive and got them back to base. After a long career in the Royal Australian Air Force, AVM Goble CBE died in Melbourne on 24 July 1948. Gamon later lived in Chester and kept in touch with his friend C P O Bartlett, who, after serving in the RAF until 1932, retired to Cheltenham and died in March 1986, aged 97.

Born in Nottingham on 10 March 1899, Lawrence Herbert Pearson joined 'Naval 2' on 18 January 1918. He was credited with six victories in DH 4s, all after his unit had become No 202 Sqn RAF, and four with 2Lt Edward Darby as his observer (*Colin Huston/Cross & Cockade International*)

DH 4 A8025 of No 202 Sqn, with two Lewis guns added to the upper wing, was flown by Lt Pearson and 2Lt Darby on 26 June 1918 when they claimed a Pfalz D IIIa OOC over Ostend, but then had to force land near Middlekercke, probably credited to Flgmstr Bottler of MFJ II. Born in Liverpool on 7 March 1888, Darby had previously downed an Albatros D III on 5 August 1917 while serving as gun layer to Flt Cdr Robert Jope-Slade of 'Naval 5'. He scored five more victories with No 202 Sqn before he and Lt C R Moore became lost in a storm over Nieuport on 28 September and were forced to land behind German lines (*Colin Huston/Cross & Cockade International*)

ATTACK AND AMALGAMATION

Arguably the most engaged RNAS fighter pilot immediately prior to the German offensive of March 1918 was Stanley Rosevear. He, Minifie and Spence each downed a Fokker Dr I on the 6th (to which Spence would subsequently add two more victories with No 201 Sqn RAF), after which Rosevear claimed another seven enemy aircraft. On the opening day of the *Kaiserschlacht* (21 March) he claimed three Albatros D Vs over Nieuport, one in flames. Given an RAF captain's rank when 'Naval 1' became No 201 Sqn, Rosevear scored thrice in April to raise his tally to 25, and received a Bar to his DSC. During a test flight on 25 April, however, his Camel failed to come out of a dive at a practice target and Rosevear died in the resulting crash.

'Naval 10's' Alexander downed a D V on 6 March and a two-seater four days later, while Mellings and Manuel each destroyed a D V on the 10th. That brought John Manuel's tally to seven, and he would raise it to 13 as a captain in No 210 Sqn prior to being killed in a midair collision with new pilot 2Lt F C Dodd on 10 June 1918.

On 8 March 'Naval 3' departed Bray-Dunes for Mont St Eloi, a few miles northeast of Arras. On the 10th Flt Sub-Lt Frederick John Shaw Britnell opened his account with the unit with a D V OOC. Born in High Wycombe, Buckinghamshire, on 16 April 1899, Britnell had joined the RNAS on 3 June 1917 and during his training days acquired the sobriquet of 'Duke', which would follow him into squadron service.

Previously misidentified as Flt Sub-Lt Ross A Blyth's Camel B5663 of 'Naval 10's' 'A' Flight, which fatally collided with Ltn Gustav Wandelt of *Jasta* 36 on 23 January 1918, this machine has recently been ascertained to be B3781, brought down near Houthulst Forest on 18 March by Ltn Emil Thuy of Royal Wurttemburg *Jasta* 28. Its pilot, Flt Sub-Lt Gordon T Steeves, spent the rest of the war in captivity (*Andrew Kemp*)

Sopwith Camel B6420 of 'Naval 1' was flown by Flt Lts Cyril B Ridley and Richard P Minifie, the latter of whom scored four victories in it. Four days after claiming two Albatros D Vs, Minifie and B6420 came down in German lines on 17 March 1918, either due to engine failure or shot down by Gefr Gebhardt of *Jasta* 47w, and he too was captured (*Bruce-Leslie Collection*)

Ray Hinchliffe of 'Naval 10' scored his second victory on 10 March when he downed a two-seater. He would add four more with No 210 Sqn until a burst tyre during a night landing caused the Camel that he was ferrying in to crash. His facial injuries included the loss of sight in his left eye, which he covered with an eyepatch thereafter. This incident did not stop Hinchcliffe from pursuing a career in aviation postwar that saw him amass more than 9000 flying hours. It came to an abrupt end on 13 March 1928, however, when he set out from Cranwell with Miss Elsie Mackay in an attempt to fly the Atlantic Ocean nonstop from east to west. They were never seen again.

Flt Cdr Rowley and Flt Sub-Lt Ridley burned a balloon at Ypres on 12 March, and Ridley would add five more to his score with No 201 Sqn, raising his personal total to 11. He also received the DSC and became a flight commander in his own right.

Dallas brought a Rumpler down in Allied lines at Dixmude on 12 March, and its crewmen, Ltn d R Horst Haustein and Ltn Ernst Stempel of FA 13, died of their wounds. Posted out of 'Naval 1' a few days later, Dallas would return as a major to command No 40 Sqn RAF in April. He had scored at least nine more victories by 1 June when his SE 5a was shot down by three triplanes of *Jasta* 14 and credited to their CO, Ltn Hans Werner. Appraisals of Dallas' final score have varied from 32 to as high as 51.

Flt Lt Minifie downed two D Vs southeast of Dixmude on 13 March, bringing his score to 21. Kinkead and Rowley each claimed a D V on the 16th, as did Findlay, along with a second in concert with Wallace. This was the latter pilot's fourth victory, and he subsequently raised his score to 14 with Nos 201 and 3 Sqns RAF.

On 17 March, Minifie went down in German lines – either due to engine failure or shot down, his machine possibly being the Camel credited to Gefr Gebhardt of *Jasta* 47w – and he was sent to Karlsrühe prison. Awarded a second Bar to his DSC a month later, Minifie joined his family's flour milling business in Australia after the war. He returned to RAF service in World War 2 as a squadron leader in the Air Training Corps and died in Melbourne on 31 March 1969.

On 21 March Hunter of 'Naval 4' destroyed a Pfalz five miles off Middelkerke, and Findlay of 'Naval 1' flamed a D V three miles southwest of Nieuport. Awarded the DSC, Findlay scored another five victories with No 201 Sqn in May, bringing his total to 14 and earning him the DFC. After further RAF service in Afghanistan and Waziristan, he became a farmer, but in October 1936 he took part in the Johannesburg Air Race, only to be killed when his Airspeed Envoy crashed while taking off in northern Rhodesia.

Rochford of 'Naval 3' described the sort of busy day that so many of his colleagues faced in the wake of the German onslaught;

'At 0921 hrs on 21 March I led my flight on an OP (offensive patrol) and we climbed to 17,000 ft. The fog had cleared and it was a sunny day, but visibility was poor and it was difficult to see the ground through the haze. After flying for about an hour I saw below us a large number of enemy aircraft, among them a red triplane, near Douai. We attacked them, and picking out an Albatros Scout I opened fire at close range and he went down out of control. I then had two more combats with Albatros Scouts, both with indecisive results. Jimmy Glen helped me to shoot down this Albatros Scout out of control and Armstrong, with "C" Flight, got another one down in the same category. The presence of the red triplane among those enemy aircraft seemed to indicate that it was von Richthofen out with his "Circus".

'In the late afternoon of that same day I led a formation of "B" and "A" Flights on an OP, flying along the lines at 17,000 ft. Near Vaulx we intercepted an Albatros two-seater. Poor chap, he had not a hope of escaping us, and we fell on him like a pack of hungry foxhounds who had caught up with their prey. Nearly all of us took part in the attack and eventually the enemy aircraft turned completely over and descended on its back in a flat spin until it hit the ground and was completely wrecked on our side of the lines.'

Credit for the two-seater was shared between Rochford, Berlyn,

Displaying 'Naval 8's' white disc squadron insignia, Camel B6290 was brought down near Lens on 22 March 1918 by Ltn Fritz Loerzer of *Jasta* 26 and the pilot, Flt Sub-Lt W S McGrath, captured (*Fleet Air Arm Museum JMB/GSL07523*)

Len Rochford (left, wearing glasses) gets an 85th birthday surprise on 10 November 1981 while attending the last World War 1 aces' reunion in Paris, where he was also reunited with 'Naval 3' squadronmate 'Nick' Carter. Rochford retained an avid interest in the history of his air war right up until his death on 17 December 1986 (*Jon Guttman*)

Chisam, Devereux, Ellwood, Hayne, Macleod and Flt Sub-Lts O P Adam and L A Sands. Rochford, whose score stood at 14, would boost his tally to 29 with No 203 Sqn RAF. When he died in Somerset on 17 December 1986, 'Titch' Rochford had left behind a rich historical legacy as an active member of the Cross & Cockade Society, a frequent commentator on his times on television and through his autobiography, *I Chose the Sky*.

Glen would score twice more in No 203 Sqn, taking his tally to 15. Serving postwar in the RCAF and the RAF, and retiring from the latter in 1938, he died in England on 7 March 1962.

Kinkead and Rowley of 'Naval 1' each claimed a D V off Nieuport on 21 March. For Kinkead, it was the 18th victory in a tally that would reach 32 by the armistice, and he would add three more successes while fighting the Bolsheviks with No 47 Sqn. He subsequently served in No 30 Sqn in Mesopotamia and Kurdistan. Kinkead then joined Britain's Schneider Trophy team, but he was killed while flying the Supermarine S 5 floatplane on 12 March 1928. Rowley scored his ninth, and final, victory on 1 April – the very day his unit became No 201 Sqn RAF. During World War 2 he served in the India-Burma theatre, rising to the rank of air commodore.

On 22 March Shook of 'Naval 4', flying Camel B6300, claimed two D Vs in flames and one OOC over Slype. One of his victims was probably Ltn zur See Bertram Heinrich of MFJ I, who was wounded. With his score at 12, Shook was awarded the DSO and CdG in 1918 and subsequently completed his RAF service as a major. He died in Bala, Ontario, on 30 May 1966.

Roy Brown of 'Naval 9' also enjoyed success on the 22nd when he destroyed a two-seater. He would score three more victories in April with No 209 Sqn RAF, his tenth, on 21 April, being widely touted to have been Rittm Manfred von Richthofen, although a multitude of studies have since attributed the 'Red Baron's' demise to ground fire. Withdrawn nine days later with influenza, as well as ulcers and shattered nerves, Brown was awarded the DFC and Bar, but he was injured in a crash on 15 July and left the RAF in April 1919 to become an accountant. After an unsuccessful attempt to join the RCAF in 1939, he then failed to secure political office in 1943. Arthur Roy Brown died of a heart attack in March of the following year.

'Naval 3' added to its tally on 23 March, with Ellwood destroying an Albatros D V and teaming up with MacLeod to get another. Whealy downed a Pfalz OOC and Armstrong also claimed one that he followed to a low altitude and saw crash near Vaulx. After 'Naval 3' became an RAF unit, Ellwood shared a tenth victory with Glen and Little on 9 April. Awarded the DSC, he remained in the RAF until 1952, becoming a Knight Commander in the Order of the Bath in 1949. Sir Aubrey Ellwood died on 20 December 1992.

On 24 March Enstone of 'Naval 4' destroyed a D V in flames for his tenth victory. As a captain in the redesignated No 204 Sqn, he would score three more and receive the DFC. That same day Alexander of 'Naval 10' downed two D Vs OOC, while Mellings claimed a Pfalz in flames and another OOC. Also claiming an Albatros in flames was Flt Sub-Lt Lawrence Percival Coombes, who had been born in India on

9 April 1899 and educated at the City of London School, before joining the RNAS in July 1917. Coombes would score 14 more victories in No 210 Sqn and enjoy a successful career in aeronautics postwar. He died in Melbourne, Victoria, on 2 June 1988.

Adding a Bar to his DSC, Capt Harold Mellings would score another five victories with No 210 Sqn and receive the DFC. After destroying a two-seater and a Fokker D VII on 22 July, however, he was killed by Ltn Ludwig Beckmann of *Jasta* 56.

Mel Alexander also scored five more victories as a captain with No 210 Sqn for a total of 22, before returning to Home Establishment with 465 combat hours in his log. As the last survivor of Collishaw's famed 'Black Flight', Alexander died in Toronto on 4 October 1988.

On 24 March 'Naval 3's' Rochford and Chisam each claimed a D V OOC near Beaumetz, and another OOC over Vaulx was shared by Armstrong's flight as his 13th, Pierce's ninth, Hayne's sixth, Whealy's 14th, Bawlf's and Berlyn's fourth and Britnell's second victory. Although wounded in the foot on 7 April, Berlyn would 'make ace' with a DFW shared with Rochford on 21 May. Bawlf would get one more on 22 July, dying in Toronto on 22 August 1966. 'Duke' Britnell had raised his score to nine by 2 October. Hayne brought his tally to 15 with No 203 Sqn, only to be killed in a flying accident in a Bristol F 2B Fighter at Castle Bromwich on 28 April 1919. Art Whealy's score totalled 27 by the time he left No 203 Sqn for Home Establishment on 24 September 1918. He would survive World War 2 as well, only to die of a heart attack while on a skiing holiday in St Marquerite, Quebec, on 23 December 1945.

Amid the fighting on 25 March, Rochford lamented, 'Now I heard the sad news that Freddy Armstrong had been killed during the morning's low flying Special Mission. The other pilots of his flight reported seeing his Camel go down in flames and crash near Ervillers'.

When Flgmstr Hans Groth of MFJ II went after an Allied balloon at 1700 hrs on 26 March, it touched off a general melee as

Camels of 'Naval 4' line up before the squadron's three hangars at St Pol-sur-Mer in March 1918. On 26 March the unit tried to foil a balloon attack that saw claims made by several 'Naval 4', Belgian and German naval aces, but which only resulted in the death of would-be balloon buster Flgmstr Hans Groth of MFJ II (*Henry Forster Album via Jon Guttman*)

A close-up of one of 'Naval 4's' Camels – whose pilot, unfortunately, is not positively identified – shows that individual markings still prevailed in the unit in March 1918, prior to its redesignation as No 204 Sqn RAF (*Henry Forster Album via Jon Guttman*)

Camels of 'Naval 4' descended on him from 17,000 ft, his cover flight intervened and Hanriot HD 1s of the Belgian *9e Escadrille* joined in. When all was over, Keirstead and Hickey each claimed a Pfalz destroyed and one OOC, Hunter was credited with another Pfalz and the Belgians made a joint claim that was later dropped. For MFJ II, Ltn zur See Theo Osterkamp and Flgmstr Eduard Blaas claimed a Camel apiece. The only known casualty was Groth, who came down at Vlaabach in Pfalz D IIIa 5923/17 and was captured, only to die of his wounds soon after.

Keirstead's double victory brought his score to 11, to which he would add two more with No 204 Sqn. Hickey would raise his tally from four to 21 with the same unit, before being killed in a midair collision with Lt S E Matthey on 3 October 1918. He was posthumously gazetted for the DSO on 2 November. Hunter's victory was his fifth, and his tally would rise to 13 with No 204 Sqn, earning him a DFC on 10 September.

While the German series of offensives continued toward their final reversal along the Marne in mid-July, the RNAS's saga abruptly ended with the stroke of a pen on 1 April 1918, as the British combined it and the RFC into a single independent air arm. All RNAS squadrons were duly renumbered in the 200 numerical range.

Most former RNAS airmen were too occupied at the time to appreciate the change, including Robert Little, who had returned to frontline service with 'Naval 3' and downed a Fokker Dr I on the day it became No 203 Sqn RAF. He brought his total to 47 on 22 May – making him Australia's ace of aces, depending on which of Stan Dallas' scores one accepts. Five days later, during an attempt to intercept a Gotha bomber on a night raid, Little's Camel was caught in a searchlight and a bullet, either from the bomber or from the ground, passed through both of his thighs. Crash-landing near Noeux, Capt Little bled to death before help could arrive.

As noted previously in their turn, a great many RNAS aces would add to or even complete their scores with the RAF, and several went on to enjoy noteworthy postwar careers. But, having amassed a proud tradition in its six years of existence, the Royal Naval Air Service had passed into history.

No 203 Sqn RAF at Izel-le-Hameau, awaiting a visit from King George V on 12 July 1918. This group shot includes a number of 'Naval 3' aces. Standing, from left to right in the back row, are Capt L D Bawlf, Lts Richard Stone, Y E S Kirkpatrick and C H Lick, Majs E T Hayne and Raymond Collishaw (CO), Capt J D Breakey, WO Hugh Neslon (engineer officer), Lts E F Adams and A E Rudge, Capts A T Whealey and H T Beamish and Lt P W Bingham (recording officer). In the front row, again from left to right, are Lts F G Black and F T S Sehl, Capt Frederick J S Britnell, Lts A W Carter, N Towell (equipment officer) and William Sidebottom, 2Lt N X Dixie, Capt L H Rochford and Lt J W Hunter (*National Archives of Canada PA2792*)

APPENDICES

RNAS Aces

Pilot	RNAS Squadron(s)	RNAS score	Total	Pilot	RNAS Squadron(s)	RNAS score	Total
W M Alexander	10	18	23	J E L Hunter	4	5	12
G B Anderson	3	5	5	P A Johnston	8	6	6
F C Armstrong	3	13	13	E G Johnstone	8	10	17
A R Arnold	3	5	5	W L Jordan	8	18	39
F E Banbury	9	11	11	R M Keirstead	4	11	13
C P O Bartlett	5	8	8	H S Kerby	3W/9/3/Walmer	9	9
H F Beamish	3	5	11	S M Kinkead	3W/1	18	35
C D Booker	8	23	29	T F Le Mesurier	5/11	7	7
L S Breadner	3	10	10	R A Little	1W/3	38	47
A R Brown	9/11/4	7	10	N M MacGregor	6/10	7	7
A W Carter	3/10	10	17	G C Mackay	13	6	18
F D Casey	2W/3	9	9	J J Malone	3W/3	10	10
A J Chadwick	5W/4	11	11	J G Manuel	10	6	13
R Collishaw	3W/3/10/13	40	60	F H M Maynard	1	6	6
R J O Compston	8	25	25	R McDonald	8	7	8
T G Culling	1	6	6	H T Mellings	2W/10	10	15
W A Curtis	6/10	13	13	R P Minifie	1W/1	21	21
R S Dallas	1W/1	23	32	H A Mott	9	5	5
H Day	10/8	11	11	R H Mulock	1W/3/82W	5	5
M J G Day	13	5	5	R B Munday	8	9	9
P M Dennett	8	5	7	G E Nash	10	6	6
B P H De Roeper	6	5	5	E W Norton	1W/6	9	9
E Dickson	10/5/205	7	14	J A Page	10	7	7
C Draper	3W/6/8	8	9	J deC Paynter	6/9/10/13	5	10
S T Edwards	3W/11/6/9	8	16	E Pierce	3/9	9	9
S E Ellis	4	5	5	J W Pinder	9/13	6	17
A B Ellwood	3	10	10	G W Price	13/8	12	12
A J Enstone	4	10	13	O W Redgate	9	10	16
C A Eyre	1	6	6	E V Reid	3W/10	19	19
J S T Fall	3/9	36	36	C B Ridley	1	6	11
M H Findlay	6/1	10	14	R H Rochford	3	14	29
D F Fitzgibbon	10	8	8	S W Rosevear	1	22	25
D M B Galbraith	1W/A/8	6	6	H V Rowley	1	8	9
T F M Gerrard	A/1	9	10	H J T Saint	10	7	7
J A Glen	3	13	15	J E Sharman	3W/10	8	8
S J Goble	1W/8/5	10	10	A M Shook	4	12	12
E R Grange	1W/8	5	5	G G Simpson	1W/8/9	8	8
E T Hayne	3	6	15	L H Slatter	SDF/13	5	7
G W Hemming	4	6	6	L F W Smith	4	8	8

Pilot	RNAS Squadron(s)	RNAS score	Total
R R Soar	5W/8	12	12
A G A Spence	1	7	9
H F Stackard	9	15	15
R R Thornely	8	9	9
G L Trapp	10	6	6
H G Travers	1W/3	5	5
A T Whealy	3W/3/9	14	27
R R Winter	6/9	5	5
A W Wood	9	11	11

Observer	RNAS Squadron	RNAS score	Total
H S Jackson	5	6	6
W Naylor	5	14	14

RNAS Pilots Who Achieved Acedom in RAF Units

Pilot	RNAS Squadron(s)	RNAS score	RAF Squadron(s)	Total
R C Berlyn	3	4	203	5
R C B Brading	1	0	201	13
J D Breakey	3	0	203	9
J S Britnell	3	2	203	9
C G Brock	1/9	3	209/3	6
C P Brown	13	1	213	14
L P Coombes	10	1	210	15
G K Cooper	8	1	208	6
E D Crundall	8	3	210	7
R H Daly	M/10	3	47	7
E B Drake	MDF	1	209	5
C G Edwards	9	0	209	6
J H Forman	6/1	4	201/70	9
J Gamon	5	2	205	7
G B Gates	1	1	201	16
R D C Gifford	RNAS	0	208	6
G H D Gossip	4	3	204	6
R Graham	SDF/13	4	213	5
W E Gray	RNAS	0	213	5
J E Green	13	2	213	15
J P Hales	9	4	209	5
F V Hall	4/8/10	4	210	6
C J Haywood	5	0	205	6
C R R Hickey	4	4	204	21
W G R Hinchliffe	10	2	210	6
R L Johns	8	4	208	9
A L Jones	10	0	210	7
S C Joseph	10	0	210	13
N Keeble	1W	2	202	6
O C Le Boutillier	9	4	209	10
C R Lupton	5	3	205	5
H B Maund	10	2	210/204	8
F J W Mellersh	9	2	209	5
W T Nash	4	0	204	8
H A Patey	10	0	210	11
C W Payton	10	0	210	11
L H Pearson	2	0	202	6
J H Siddall	RNAS Dunkirk	0	209	9
C J Sims	13	0	213	9
H C Smith	RNAS	0	213	5
W H Sneath	8	4	208	5
E Swale	10	0	210	17
R Sykes	9/3	1	203	6
M S Taylor	9	1	209	7
A H Turner	RNAS	0	204/213	5
A G Warren	6	0	206	8
J B White	8	2	208	12

RNAS Observers Who Achieved Acedom in RAF units

Observer	RNAS Squadron(s)	Score	RAF Squadron(s)	Total
E B C Betts	2	1	202	6
L A Christian	6	0	206	9
E Darby	5	1	202	6
S F Langstone	5	0	205	5
W J Middleton	5	1	205	6
C V Robinson	5	1	205	7
W H Scott	5	1	205	8

COLOUR PLATES

Artist Harry Dempsey has created the colour profiles for this volume, working closely with the author to portray the aircraft as accurately as circumstances permit. Some of the illustrations are, admittedly, reconstructions based on fragmentary photographic evidence or descriptions provided by the pilots while they were alive, combined with known unit marking policy.

1
Nieuport 11 3992 of Flt Sub-Lt Redford Henry Mulock, 'A' Naval Squadron, 1 Naval Wing, Dunkirk, Belgium, May 1916

'Red' Mulock was credited with two enemy aeroplanes OOC and one 'forced to land' when flying Nieuport 3992, and he claimed two more two-seaters OOC off Nieuport on 21 May 1916. Although his off-cited status as the RNAS' – and Canada's – first ace rests unsteadily upon aerial victory criteria that later became stricter, Mulock's indisputable aggressiveness against shipping and submarines, as well as aircraft, earned him the DSO in June. Canadian squadronmate Flt Sub-Lt Daniel Murray Bayne Galbraith was also flying 3992 when he claimed a floatplane in flames off Ostend on 28 September for his second of six victories.

2
Triplane N5431 of Flt Sub-Lt Harold T Mellings, 2 Naval Wing, Mudros, Eastern Mediterranean, September 1917

The only Triplane in the Mediterranean, N5431 crash-landed at an airstrip on the edge of Mikra Bay, near Salonika, on 26 March 1917. The pilot, Flt Lt John W Alcock, survived to achieve postwar fame by making the first nonstop flight across the Atlantic Ocean on 14-15 June 1919. N5431 was rebuilt with the serial obscured, and Alcock added a Lewis gun to fire over the propeller at an angle. Flt Sub-Lt H T Mellings, with a previous victory in a Bristol Scout on 30 September 1916, used N5431 to shoot down an Albatros W 4 floatplane fighter near Mudros on 30 September 1917, followed by an Albatros D III on 19 November, a Rumpler in flames six days later and another D III on 29 November. Awarded the DSC and the Greek War Cross, Mellings later flew Camels over the Western Front with 'Naval 10' and its RAF successor, No 210 Sqn, scoring ten more victories and adding a Bar to his DSC, as well as the DFC. After destroying a two-seater and a Fokker D VII on 22 July 1918, Mellings was shot down and killed by Ltn Ludwig Beckmann of *Jasta* 56 whilst patrolling over Ostend.

3
Sopwith 1½ Strutter 9407 of Flt Sub-Lt Raymond Collishaw, 3 Naval Wing, Luxeuil-les-Bains, France, October 1916

While flying Sopwith 1½ Strutter 9407 as an escort fighter with 3 Naval Wing, Ray Collishaw took part on the Oberndorf bombing raid of 12 October 1916, the raid on Hagendingen on the 23rd and claimed two enemy scouts on 25 October. Flt Cdr Christopher Draper, with Sub-Lt L V Pearkes in 9407's observer's pit, was credited with a Fokker biplane and a two-seater OOC on 10 November and an enemy aeroplane destroyed two weeks later, this time with Sub-Lt Barker as his observer. Another future ace, Flt Sub-Lt Ellis V Reid, flew 9407 during the 16 March 1917 raid on Mörchingen aerodrome. The war-weary aircraft was eventually returned to St Pol depot on 26 April and deleted on 19 June 1917.

4
Sopwith 1½ Strutter N5088 of Flt Sub-Lt John E Sharman, 'Red' Naval Squadron, 3 Naval Wing, Ochey, France, January 1917

Having joined 3 Naval Wing by October 1916, single-seat 1½ Strutter N5088 was flown on seven missions by Flt Sub-Lt Ambrose B Shearer, who had a Lewis gun fitted above the upper wing centre section in November but never got the opportunity to use it. On 25 February the aircraft was flown by Flt Sub-Lt John Sharman in a bombing raid on the blast furnaces at Brebach. 'Shortly after leaving the objective I observed two Fokker monoplanes coming in from the right at some distance', he reported. 'They finally came in touch with our right wing. With Flt Sub-Lt H Edwards in another bomber, I closed with the leader. After 20 rounds from the Vickers he suddenly dived very steeply and I lost sight of him, as I was only about 100 ft distant from him at the time and he disappeared under my wing'. Flt Sub-Lts Edwards and C B deT Drummond confirmed the Eindecker as 'OOC'. On 19 April 1917 N5088 was presented to the French, and ten days later Sharman was transferred to 'Naval 10'.

5

Triplane N5425 of Flt Sub-Lt Herbert V Rowley, 1 Naval Squadron, La Bellevue, France, April 1917

Victor Rowley used N5425 to claim his first aerial success – an Albatros D III OOC near Villers le Cagnicourt in concert with Flt Sub-Lt Cyril B Ridley – on 29 April 1917. He went on to score four more victories in Triplanes and four in Camels, the last of which (an Albatros D V OOC over Arras-Albert) was claimed on the very day that his unit became No 201 Sqn RAF – 1 April 1918. Flt Sub-Lt Stanley W Rosevear also flew N5425 on occasion, but he did not score any of his 25 victories in it.

6

Camel B6420 of Flt Cdr Richard P Minifie, 1 Naval Squadron, St-Eloi, France, March 1918

Depicted with provisionally reconstructed colours, Camel B6420 was flown by Flt Cdr Richard Pearson Minifie while serving as acting commander of 'Naval 1' following the departure of Flt Lt R S Dallas while Flt Lt C D Booker was still on leave. With 17 previous victories scored in Triplanes, Minifie used B6420 to claim an Albatros D V OOC on 29 November, to destroy a DFW C V on 8 December and down two D Vs on 13 March. Four days later, however, B6420 came down in German lines – either due to engine failure or after having been attacked by Gefr Gebhardt of *Jasta* 47w – and Minifie spent the rest of the war in Karlsrühe prison.

7

Pup N6160 *BLACK MARIA* of Flt Lt Raymond Collishaw, 3 Naval Squadron, Marieux, France, March 1917

N6160 was assigned to Flt Lt Collishaw in 'C' Flight, all of whose Pups, according to Len Rochford, had black cowlings and names such as his own *BLACK BESS* (N6207), Flt Cdr Robin Mack's *BLACK TULIP*, Art Whealy's *BLACK PRINCE* and Edmund Pierce's *N6171 BLACK ARROW*. While flying N6160, Collishaw claimed Halberstadt D IIs OOC on 15 February and 4 March 1917, although he left 'Naval 3' soon afterwards with a case of frostbite. 'It is reported that Collishaw, when he became Flight Commander of "B" Flight in 10 Naval Squadron, had the cowlings of his Triplanes painted black and named his machine *BLACK MARIA*', Rochford noted 'As a result the flight soon became known as "Black Flight"'.

8

Pup N6179 *BABY MINE* of Flt Sub-Lt A W Carter, 3 Naval Squadron, Marieux, France, April 1917

Shown with the red cowling of 'B' Flight, N6179 was assigned to 'Naval 3' in February and flown by Flt Cdr T C Vernon and then Nick Carter, who scored two victories in it on 23 April and another on the 29th. It was later reassigned to 'C' Flight and the cowling painted black. N6179 subsequently served with the Seaplane Defence Flight at Dunkirk and a Home Defence squadron at Manston, in Kent.

9

Pup N6162 *"I WONDER"* of Flt Sub-Lt Leonard H Rochford, 3 Naval Squadron, Furnes, Belgium, July 1917

Bearing the blue cowling and wheels of 'A' Flight, N6162 was flown on 11 May 1917 by Flt Sub-Lt Hubert S Broad, who had three victories to his name when he was driven down by Ltn Adolf *Ritter* von Tutschek of *Jasta* 12. Although one bullet entered Broad's open mouth as he was looking back and exited through his chin, he managed to spin down, recover and force land near Bapaume in Allied lines. Later given an overwing Lewis gun and christened *"I WONDER"*, this Pup was being 'borrowed' by 'Titch' Rochford of 'C' Flight when he and four other pilots shared in the downing of a German floatplane six miles north of Ostend on 7 July 1917. Rochford's fourth victory, and the next 25 after that, would be in Camels. N6162 was subsequently flown by Flt Sub-Lt William H Chisam, who joined the squadron in August 1917, but he would score all seven of his victories in Camels between 3 September 1917 and 24 March 1918.

10

Camel N6377 of Flt Sub-Lt Harold F Beamish, 3 Naval Squadron, Furnes, Belgium, September 1917

Typifying the colourful markings sported in naval units before the RAF standardised more sober ones, N6377, with its fern leaf on the upper decking, reflected the nationality of its pilot, Harold Francis Beamish, who was born in Havelock North, New Zealand, on 7 July 1896, and joined the RNAS in June 1916. Assigned to 'Naval 3' on 9 January 1917, 'Kiwi' Beamish was flying Camel N6377 on 27 July when he and four squadronmates destroyed a German floatplane 20 miles off Ostend. He also flew N6377 on 5 September, when he despatched an Albatros D V OOC, on the 10th when he and four other pilots brought down a DFW C V near their airfield (the crew, Vfw Friedrich Eckhardt and Ltn Franz Adolf Gilge of FA (A) 293b were captured) and on the 23rd, when he claimed another Albatros OOC. N6377 later served with 'Naval 8', where Flt Sub-Lt Edward Grahame Johnstone scored six of his 17 victories in it between 19 January and 3 February 1918.

11

Camel N6347 of Flt Lt Alexander M Shook, 4 Naval Squadron, Bray Dunes, France, June 1917

Arriving at 'Naval 4' in late May 1917, Camel N6347 was flown by Flt Cdr Shook when he attacked an enemy aeroplane 15 miles off Nieuport on 4 June. Although this machine escaped, the next evening Shook engaged 15 German aircraft between Nieuport and Ostend, sending a scout crashing on the beach and driving a two-seater down

OOC. These were the first Camel victories, and when added to three that Shook had previously scored in Pup N6200, they made him an ace. Flying N6363, Shook downed three more enemy aircraft prior to being wounded on 21 October. After returning to 'Naval 4', he raised his total to 12 in March 1918.

12

DH 4 N6000 of 5 Naval Squadron, Petite Synthe, France, February 1918

Standing out among the bombers that fought their way to and from their targets in Flanders, N6000 was crewed by Capt Charles R Lupton and AGL Smith when they downed an Albatros D V on 8 December 1917. New Zealander Euan Dickson and Walter Naylor crewed it when they were credited with Albatros D Vs on 17 and 18 February 1918. Flt Lt C P O Bartlett, who regarded N6000 as his favourite aeroplane, was in it when he and Naylor claimed a Fokker Dr I OOC on 21 March and an Albatros OOC on 27 March. After the unit was redesignated No 205 Sqn RAF, Capt Lupton and Gunner Albert G Wood downed a Pfalz D IIIa OOC on N6000 on 7 April. On the 17th, however, they were shot up by fighters and forced to land with N6000's rudder controls disabled, their demise being credited to either Ltn Johannes Jensen or Uffz Otto Wieprich of *Jasta* 57. Lupton and Wood were unhurt, but both were killed in action on 9 May 1918.

13

Nieuport 17bis N3208 of Flt Cdr Ernest W Norton, 6 Naval Squadron, Flez, France, April 1917

Previously credited with a balloon while with 'A' Naval Squadron of 1 Naval Wing, Ernest Norton became 'Naval 6's' most successful fighter pilot, starting with an Aviatik OOC on 8 February, two Albatros D IIs west of Douai on 3 April and two D IIIs (one shared with Flt Sub-Lt Alfred L Thorne) six days later. As 'C' Flight leader, Norton flew Nieuport N3208 from 22 through 29 April, and on the latter date he and Flt Sub-Lt Albert H V Fletcher shared in driving a scout out of control at Honnecourt in the afternoon. This may have been the aircraft flown by Ltn Hermann Göring of *Jasta* 26, who made it home with his rudder controls shot away. Later that same evening Norton claimed a scout in flames and another OOC near Guise. This 'hat trick' brought his total to nine victories. Sqn Cdr Charles D Breese was flying N3208 on 1 June when he and Flt Sub-Lt Arthur McBurney Walton shared in driving a two-seater down OOC at St Quentin.

14

Nieuport 17bis N3101 of Flt Cdr Christopher Draper, 6 Naval Squadron, Flez, France, June 1917

Bearing two red bands, but with an unpainted cowl and wheel covers, N3101 was flown by the 'B' Flight leader when he claimed an Albatros scout OOC and another destroyed northwest of Cambrai on 6 June 1917. Ironically, complaints in the squadron of Draper being better at stunting over the aerodrome and leading drinking parties than at effectively commanding his flight had already set the wheels in motion for his withdrawal to Home Establishment on 11 June. At the end of July, however, Draper returned to the front with 'Naval 8', taking command of the unit in September. Flying Camels, he drove an Albatros D V down OOC on 11 September and shared in burning a balloon with Flt Cdr

R B Munday on 3 October. His final claim, which came after his unit had became No 208 Sqn RAF, took the form of a DFW C V two-seater reconnaissance aircraft despatched OOC on 8 May. Awarded the DFC, Draper wrote an autobiography, *The Mad Major*, in the 1950s and died on 16 January 1979.

15

Pup N5194 of Flt Sub-Lt E Rochford Grange, 8 Naval Squadron, Vert Galand, France, January 1917

Aside from a few personal names, which proliferated later on its Triplanes, 'Naval 8's' Nieuports and Pups were devoid of markings. Canadian-born, American-trained Flt Sub-Lt 'Roch' Grange, who had scored the second Pup victory on 25 September 1916, flew N5194 when he was credited with an Albatros D II shot down and two OOC on 4 January 1917, but lost Flt Sub-Lt Allan S Todd, killed by Ltn Manfred *Freiherr* von Richthofen of *Jasta* 'Boelcke', in the same action. Three days later Grange scored his fifth victory over another *Jasta* 'Boelcke' D II, which he sent down OOC over Grevillers despite suffering a painful wound in his right shoulder. Flt Sub-Lt Robert A Little also scored his fourth victory on 7 January. Grange, who spent the rest of the war as an instructor, lived long enough to attend the last international aces' reunion in Paris in 1981, before dying in Toronto on 13 July 1988.

16

Triplane N5464 *DORIS* of Flt Sub-Lt Edward D Crundall, 8 Naval Squadron, St-Eloi, France, April 1917

Born on 9 December 1896 and a member of the RNAS since 1914, E D Crundall scored his first victories (two Albatros two-seaters OOC near Henin-Liétard) while flying N5464 on 14 April 1917. He was shot down with wounds in Allied lines on 10 May, having fallen victim to future German ace Ltn Aloys Heldmann of *Jasta* 10 – the latter was only credited with an unconfirmed 'probable'. On 18 August he, Booker and Munday drove down an Albatros D V OOC. Crundall subsequently scored four more victories in Camels with No 210 Sqn RAF.

17

Triplane N5493 of Flt Lt Robert A Little, 8 Naval Squadron, St-Eloi, France, May-July 1917

Nicknamed *BLYMP* after Little's son, N5493 became the most successful single Triplane after Ray Collishaw's N5492 *BLACK MARIA* of 'Naval 10'. Indeed, Little scored 20 victories in it between 29 April and 10 July 1917. His ultimate tally of 47 by 22 May 1918 made him the leading Australian ace of all time, but on the night of 27 May 1918 Little died of wounds suffered while trying to intercept a Gotha bomber.

18

Triplane N6292 *LILY* of Flt Sub-Lt Reginald R Soar, 8 Naval Squadron, St-Eloi, France, May-July 1917

Often flying wingman to Bob Little, Reggie Soar flew Pup N6181 when he claimed his first victories (two Halberstadt D IIs OOC) on 20 December 1916. Of the ten victories he scored thereafter, six were achieved whilst at the controls of Triplane N6292 between 23 May and 22 July 1917. In between those successes, Soar used a Camel to share in the destruction of a pair of two-seaters on 11 and 13 July.

19

Camel B3757 of Flt Cdr Philip A Johnston, 8 Naval Squadron, St-Eloi, France, July 1917

Distinguished only by a red and white band, Camel B3757 was flown by Phil Johnston to bring down two two-seaters OOC on 13 July 1917 and an Albatros D III destroyed nine days later – these victories took his tally to six. Johnston was also flying B3757 on 17 August when he fatally collided with Flt Sub-Lt B A Bennetts' Camel B3877 during a melee over Wingles, both pilots being credited to Oblt Hans Bethge of *Jasta* 30.

20

Triplane N5482 of Flt Cdr Charles D Booker, 8 Naval Squadron, St-Eloi, France, August 1917

Shown with the white fuselage roundel surround introduced in July 1917, N5482 was flown by C D Booker. He claimed his first victory in it on 26 April, and would add 13 more by 11 August. His victim on the latter date was none other than Oblt Adolf *Ritter* von Tutschek, commander of *Jasta* 12 and then victor over 22 Allied aeroplanes, who was brought down severely wounded. Booker scored once more in Triplane N5460 on 18 August and then permanently switched to Camels. Having brought his total to 29 on 13 August 1918 with three Fokker D VIIs downed in just a matter of minutes, Booker was then fatally wounded by Ltn Ulrich Neckel – yet another *Jasta* 12 ace.

21

Camel B3921 of Flt Cdr Richard B Munday, 8 Naval Squadron, St-Eloi, France, November 1917

Born in Plymouth on 31 January 1896, Richard Burnard Munday was a medical student before the war, later joining the RNAS and earning his RAC No 1085 licence at Brooklands on 16 February 1915. In 1916 Sub Flt-Lt Munday served as an instructor on Curtiss JN-4s at Cranwell – where his pupils included future ace Leonard Rochford – before getting a combat assignment to 'Naval 8' in the summer of 1917. His first victory (an Albatros OOC with Flt Cdr C D Booker and Flt Sub-Lt E D Crundall) on 19 August was scored in Triplane N5421. Munday was flying Camel B3921 when he burned a kite balloon at Query la Motte at 2000 hrs on 2 September. He destroyed another balloon in its shed at Brebières at 2200 hrs on the 29th, shared in the destruction of a third one with Sqn Cdr Christopher Draper at Douai at 2300 hrs on 3 October and disposed of a fourth north of Meurchin at 0610 hrs on 7 November. Munday had switched to Camel B6378 by the time he 'roasted' his fifth 'sausage' at 1900 hrs on 21 January 1918, drove down an Albatros D V OOC on the 29th and similarly downed another on 3 February. His ninth victory (a two-seater OOC near Drocourt) came on 21 February. Munday was awarded the DSC for his performance with 'Naval 8' and subsequently became a major in the RAF.

22

Camel B3883 of Flt Sub-Lt Oliver C Le Boutillier, 9 Naval Squadron, Leffrinckhoucke, France, August 1917

The RNAS's only American ace, New Jersey-born Oliver Colin Le Boutillier had scored four victories in Triplanes with 'Naval 9' from 26 May through to 29 July 1917 before being issued with Camel B3883 on 4 August – only to 'crack it up' ten days

later. Repaired, the aircraft was returned to the squadron on 10 September, and between the 11th and 30th Flt Sub-Lt Harold F Stackard scored at least six victories in it. Flt Lt Joe Fall also used B3883 to down an Albatros D V OOC on 4 November and to destroy two Albatros two-seaters on the 13th. Reassigned to training duties on 31 December, B3883 was finally written off in a crash at Manston on 27 April 1918. 'Boots' Le Boutillier went on to be credited with a further six enemy aeroplanes whilst at the controls of Camel D3338 with No 209 Sqn RAF.

23

Camel B3898 *DORIS* of Flt Lt Joseph S T Fall, 9 Naval Squadron, Leffrinckhoucke, France, October 1917

In July 1917 Canadian Joe Fall was credited with eight victories and was awarded the DFC while serving with 'Naval 3'. He was then posted to 'Naval 9' as a flight leader, consequently giving him carte blanche when it came to applying markings to his assigned Camel, B3898. Fall scored 11 victories in this aircraft between 3 September and 31 October 1917, after which it was returned to the Northern Aircraft Park on 3 November.

24

Camel B3884 of Flt Lt Alfred W Wood, 9 Naval Squadron, Leffrinckhoucke, France, September 1917

Born in Heaton, West Yorkshire, on 9 April 1898, Wood enlisted in the RNAS on 15 October 1916, trained in 12 Naval Squadron in August 1917 and was then posted to 'Naval 9'. A quick learner, he would claim eight enemy aeroplanes in the month of September alone, five of them in B3884. Wood added two more to his tally in this machine on 13 November and 10 December. All of his 11 victories were shared with squadronmates. B3884 would later serve with No 201 Sqn RAF, and Capt Maxwell Hutcheon Findlay was flying it when he scored two of his 14 victories – the shared destruction of an Albatros D V on 15 May 1918 and a D V despatched OOC two days later.

25

Camel B3893 of Flt Lt Arthur Roy Brown, 9 Naval Squadron, Leffrinckhoucke, France, September 1917

During 'Naval 9's' decorative period, 'A' Flight had the face of music hall comedian and popularly styled 'Prime Minister of Mirth' George Robey cut from advertising placards for the show *Zigzag* and doped onto the left vertical stabilisers of its Camels. Flt Lt Roy Brown flew B3893 when he drove a two-seater down OOC on 17 September, destroyed a DFW C V in flames near Ostend on the 20th and downed an Albatros D V OOC on 28 October for his sixth victory. Carrying on in No 209 Sqn RAF, Brown's tenth, and last, victory was a Fokker Dr I on 21 April 1918, popularly identified, in spite of evidence to the contrary, as having been flown by *Rittm* Manfred von Richthofen.

26

Triplane N6302 of Flt Lt Alfred W Carter, 10 Naval Squadron, Droglandt, France, July 1917

Born in Calgary, Alberta, on 29 April 1894, Nick Carter was assigned to 3 Naval Wing in 1916 and scored his first five victories flying Pups with 'Naval 3' between 6 April and

27 May 1917. Posted to 'Naval 10' as 'A' Flight leader in July, Carter, in spite of a self-professed fear of Triplanes, used N6302 to drive Albatros D Vs down OOC on the 17th, 23rd, 24th and 27th of that month. When Flt Lt W M Alexander relieved Carter as 'A' Flight leader, he 'inherited' N6302, with which he downed D Vs on 20 and 21 August. Flying Camels, Carter downed a D V on 19 February 1918 and added five more aeroplanes and a balloon to his tally after 'Naval 10' became No 210 Sqn RAF.

27
Triplane N6307 of Flt Sub-Lt John Sharman, 10 Naval Squadron, Droglandt, France, July 1917
N6307, depicted as BLACK DEATH in Norman Franks' Osprey Aircraft of the Aces 62 – Sopwith Triplane Aces of World War 1 book, did not look like that for long. John Sharman transferred to 'C' Flight on 4 June 1917 and flew N6307 with a blue engine cowling, wheels and vertical stabiliser. He scored most of his eight victories thereafter and later commanded 'C' Flight, but was killed in N6307 on 22 July.

28
Camel B6202 of Flt Lt Desmond F Fitzgibbon, 10 Naval Squadron, Droglandt, France, September 1917
Reconstructed as it would have looked when Flt Lt Fitzgibbon – then one of 'Naval 10's' few remaining pilots boasting combat experience – was leading 'B' Flight in September, with bands extended over the upper decking to signify his flight leader's status, B6202 was used by him to down Albatros D Vs OOC on 14, 26 and 27 September 1917. The aircraft was passed on to Fitzgibbon's deputy, Flt Sub-Lt Wilfred A Curtis, when he was placed in command of 'A' Flight on 15 October, and used by him to score or share in seven victories by 15 November. After the squadron's return from 'disgraced exile on the Flanders coast' to 4 Naval Wing at Teteghem aerodrome on 20 November, 'Naval 10's' mechanics, as a morale-boosting measure, began adorning its Camels with stripes along either side of the cowling – black and white for 'A' Flight, red and white for 'B' and blue and white for 'C'. There is no evidence that B6202 was so marked, however, and when it was issued to Flt Cdr W M Alexander upon his return from Canadian leave to resume charge of 'C' Flight on 4 January 1918, he adamantly refused to have anything other than the command bands and flight letter on his machine! Alexander never scored in B6202, however, his next success (a D V OOC on 23 January) coming in B6289 and the seven after that in B7215.

29
Baby N1019 PHYLLIS of Flt Sub-Lt Ronald Graham, Seaplane Defence Flight, St Pol-sur-Mer, June 1917
While covering the North Sea Fleet with the SDF at St Pol, Ronnie Graham named his Blackburn-built Sopwith Baby N1019 after his girlfriend, Nurse Phyllis Farmer. Flying N1016 on 19 June 1917, Graham and a second Baby were escorting a Short 184 when they came under attack from three floatplanes of German Seeflugstation II ten miles north-northeast of Nieuport. The other two British floatplanes were shot down, but Graham despatched one of the Germans and then alighted alongside a French destroyer and directed its crew to assist the casualties on both sides. Put in command

of the flight on 30 June, Graham remained with the SDF when it was redesignated as 13 Naval Squadron, downing a floatplane in a Pup on 12 August and two more in Camels on 15 and 25 September. After recovering from a crash suffered on 29 December – while stunting for Miss Farmer – Maj Graham returned to command what had become No 213 Sqn RAF in May 1918, and he scored his fifth victory over an LVG on 19 October.

BIBLIOGRAPHY

Bartlett, C P O, Bomber Pilot — 1917-1918, Ian Allan Ltd, Shepperton, Surrey, 1974

Black, Charles, 'Harold Francis Beamish DSC', Cross & Cockade Journal (International), Vol 19, No 4, pp 196-201

Carter, A W, letters to author, 24 April and 14 May 1980 and 9 January and 15 February 1982

Franks, Norman, Bloody April . . . Black September, Grub Street, London, 1995

Franks, Norman, Osprey Aircraft of the Aces 67 - Sopwith Pup Aces of World War 1, Osprey, Botley, Oxford, England, 2005

Franks, Norman, Osprey Aircraft of the Aces 62 - Sopwith Triplane Aces of World War 1, Osprey, Botley, Oxford, England, 2004

Franks, Norman, Sharks Among the Minnows, Grub Street, London, 2001

Franks, Norman, Bailey, Frank and Duiven, Rick, The Jasta War Chronology, Grub Street, London, 1998

Franks, Norman, Gilpin, Hal and McCrery, Nigel, Under the Guns of the Red Baron, Grub Street, London, 1995

Grange, E Rochford, letter to author, 25 May 1982

Hadingham, Evan, The Fighting Triplanes, The MacMillan Company, New York, NY, 1968

Pearson, Bob, '. . . More Than Could Be Reasonably Anticipated', The Story of No 3 Naval Wing', Over the Front, Vol 13, No 4, Winter 1998, pp 292-331

Pierce, Edmund, 'Recollections of Naval 3 and Naval 9', Cross & Cockade (USA) Journal, Vol 23, No 3, Summer 1982, pp 193-214

Rochford, Leonard H, I Chose the Sky, William Kimber & Co, Ltd, London, 1977

Rochford, Leonard H, letter to author, 11 December 1981

Shores, Christopher, Franks, Norman and Guest, Russell, Above the Trenches, Grub Street, London, 1990

Soar, Reginald Rhys, 'Robert Alexander Little', Cross & Cockade (USA) Journal, Vol 16, No 2, Summer 1975, pp 168-170

von Tutschek, Adolf Ritter, 'The War Letters of Hptmn Adolf Ritter von Tutschek', Over the Front, Vol 4, No 1, Spring 1989, pp 9-10

Westrop, Mike, A History of No 6 Sqn Royal Navy Air Servce in World War I, Schiffer Military History, Atglen, PA, 2006

Westrop, Mike, A History of No 10 Sqn Royal Navy Air Service in World War I, Schiffer Military History, Atglen, PA, 2004

Whetton, Douglass, 'When All Roads Led to France - The Story of Captain Robert Alexander Little DSO, DSC', Cross & Cockade Great Britain Journal, Vol 7, No 1, Spring 1976, pp 13-21

INDEX

References to illustrations are shown in **bold**. Plates are shown with page and caption locators in brackets.